CHINA
THROUGH
LOOKING

博爱之都

A Cultural and Historical Guide for Travelers

NANJING

Roy Kesey

Atomic Energy Press

Acknowledgements
（特别鸣谢）

For a great many different sorts of assistance, my thanks go to: Eric Abrahamsen, Chaos Chen, Robert Daly, Fu Banghua, Gu Qian, Han Dong, Jonathan Keller, Jenny Li, Lu Yang, Joy Ma, Julie Sisk, Sun Jianchun, Tang Guo, Brian Wallace, Wang Bin, Pauline Yao, Zhang Lijia, Zhang Xianwen, Zhong Xunzheng, Zhou Daoxiang, and the Nanjing Bureau of Tourism. My thanks also to the authors who kindly permitted me to quote from their work: Simon Winchester, Gavin Menzies, Peter Hessler, Kerk Phillips, Mark Alexander, and the National Gallery of Art in Washington, D.C. Special thanks go to David Hinton for permission to quote from his translation of the Xie Lingyun poem from which the epigraph of this book is drawn, and to Josh Stenberg for, among other things, his translation of the lyrics cited from *The Peach Blossom Fan.*

All these things--
it's their singularity that makes them noble
together, each at ease in its own seasons.
-Xie Lingyun, "Dwelling in the Mountains"

谢灵运《山居赋》

《深度看中国·南京》序一

中国国家旅游局副局长 顾朝曦

中国是世界闻名的四大文明古国之一，历史悠久、文化博大精深；幅员辽阔，江山秀丽多骄，旅游资源之多、秉赋之高，世界公认。今天的中国旅游业，已经由一个旅游资源大国发展成为市场最具活力，且潜力巨大的世界旅游大国，成了世界瞩目的国际旅游目的地和客源地。

南京是中国著名的四大古都之一，人杰地灵，文脉深远，东吴、东晋、宋、齐、梁、陈、南唐、明、太平天国、中华民国等10个政权相继在此建都，有“六朝古都”和“十朝都会”之称，亦有“江南佳丽地，金陵帝王州”之说，是中国近代史影响最大的城市之一。南京横跨长江南北，西望三峡，东去上海，境内山水环抱，是长江三角洲上美丽的绿都，拥有得天独厚的旅游资源，旅游市场十分广阔，近年来旅游业保持了较快的增长势头，已成为海外朋友来中国华东地区旅游的主要目的地之一。为了更好地向海外朋友介绍南京，南京市旅游局创新旅游推广方式，专门邀请了美国旅行作家Roy Kesey先生编写了这本《外国人看南京》一书，以外国人的视角来诠释南京的灿烂文化和秀丽风景。我相信，此书会让海外朋友更好地认识南京，更多地来南京及华东地区观光旅游。

旅游是和平的语言，友谊的桥梁，是当今世界增进理解、促进和谐的重要力量。中国旅游业正在为构建和谐世界、和谐社会而不懈努力。作为世界公认的最安全的旅游目的地，中国热诚欢迎世界各国、各地的朋友来中国观光旅游。

顾朝曦

二〇〇七年二月十四日

Preface

China Through the Looking Glass, Nanjing

In recent years, Nanjing's tourism industry has maintained a steady and impressive rate of growth, and the city has become one of the main tourist destinations in eastern China for travelers visiting from abroad. In order to introduce Nanjing to the world, the Nanjing tourism bureau has blazed a new trail by inviting the American writer Roy Kesey to write this book, *China Through the Looking Glass: Nanjing.* In it, he interprets the ancient culture and radiant scenery of Nanjing through a foreigner's eyes. I believe that through this book, more and more travelers will come to know of Nanjing, and choose it and the other cities of eastern China as their travel destination.

Tourism is a bridge of peace and friendship, and it is also an important force for enhancing understanding and promoting harmony. China's tourism industry is trying to help build a harmonious society, and as the safest tourism destination in the world, China cordially welcomes visitors from all over.

Gu Zhaoxi

Vice President

China National Tourism Association

February 14, 2007

《深度看中国·南京》序二
南京市人民政府副市长 陈刚

美国知名作家 Roy Kesey 找到我，问我对南京这座城市印象最深的是什么。我的回答是：古韵深邃的历史文化。

我赴南京就职尚未满一年，已经深深地爱上了这座城市。不仅是它山环水绕、风光旖旎，更主要的是有着 2479 年的建城史。在这漫漫的历史长河中，出现过多少人物，发生过多少事件，让人感动，让人唏嘘，让人拍案，让人反思……

抚摸着南京城墙城砖上烧制的文字。它们似乎在倾诉着什么。这个600年前建筑的砖石城墙，全长35.267公里，比法国巴黎的城墙要长6公里多，居世界第一。如今，它仍有三分之二遗存着，其保护的规模仍居世界首位。城市在不断拓展。它已不再是围墙，而是在城市中心位置环抱。城市因它而骄傲，它却默默宽容地看着城市的一切变迁。

如果要用几个词来概括我们的这座城市，可以称它：六朝古都，十朝都城，人文绿都，璀璨金陵，世界第一城垣……

我很欣赏Roy Kesey选择南京来写一座城市。在与他的交谈中，我也能感觉到，打动他的同样是这座城市的历史和文化。他曾两次来南京采风，深入到城市的旮旮旯旯，探寻文化遗存，又访问了不少当地知名作家、历史学家、艺术家及生活在其中的外国人，采集了许多鲜活的第一手资料。未曾料到，他到南京寻找并拜访的第一人，是78岁高龄的建筑大师、也是南京长江大桥桥头堡的设计者钟训正老先生。他一眼就相中了这位极具人文南京色彩的当代人物，可见作家独特的思考和敏锐的捕捉力。

Roy Kesey 在美国曾获文学、哲学、艺术学的学位，也曾在法国、秘鲁等国讲学，并一直从事着文学创作。他既读千卷书，又行万里路，现在又用他本国的文字来描绘中国的一座历史悠久的城市，一定是在做一件很有意思的事。应该说，他选择了写南京，南京同样也选择了由他执笔，无疑都是明智之举。

现在，Roy Kesey 的这本书即将付梓出版。这是第一部外国作家写游览南京的书。我由衷地表示祝贺，并希望众多的外国人能看到这本书，从中认识南京，了解南京，进而读懂南京，而且能来亲身体验一下南京。

祝愿广大的读者，成为南京的朋友。

A note from the Deputy Mayor of the Nanjing People's Government: Chen Gang

Roy Kesey, a well-known American writer, recently asked me what aspect of Nanjing made the deepest impression on me. My answer was: its profound cultural history.

Less than a year after coming to Nanjing, I have already fallen deeply in love with this city. Not only with the stirring mountains and gentle waters which surround it, but also with its 2479 years of urban history. During the long course of this history, how many great figures and events have manifested themselves, have moved us, made us sigh or strike the table, made us think...

I touch the words seared into the bricks of Nanjing's city wall, and they speak to me. This 600-year-old wall of brick and stone stretches out 35.267 kilometers, six kilometers longer than the Paris city wall, making it the longest such wall in the world. Two-thirds of it still remains today, and our wall preservation efforts are the most rigorous in the world. The city continues to expand, and the wall no longer encloses it, but it still encircles the city's heart. The city is proud of its wall, and the wall silently accepts all the changes of the city.

If Nanjing could be captured in only a few words, they would be: the ancient seat of six dynasties, the capital city of ten dynasties, a jewel of nature and culture, the world's greatest city wall...

I am gratified that Roy Kesey has chosen Nanjing as the subject of his book.

I can tell through our conversations that the same things that move me move him as well—the city's history and culture. He has twice visited Nanjing to collect material, venturing into every corner of the city in search of cultural remnants. Having interviewed many well-known local writers, historians, artists and foreigners, Roy has amassed a quantity of living firsthand materials. Who knew that the first person he intended to interview would be a 78-year-old architect, the great designer of the bridgehead of the Yangtze River Bridge, Mr. Zhong Xunzheng. That Roy settled so swiftly on a living personage who so uniquely represents Nanjing's culture shows the uniqueness of his thought and insight.

Roy Kesey has studied literature, philosophy and art. He has lectured in France, Peru, the United States and other countries, and has devoted himself to literary creation. He has traveled extensively and done a great deal of research, and now has described a Chinese city with a very long history—an undertaking of great significance. He has chosen to write about Nanjing and Nanjing has chosen him to do the writing; no doubt both have chosen wisely.

I sincerely congratulate Roy Kesey on the publication of this book, and I hope it finds its way into the hands of foreign friends—that it helps them to come to know Nanjing, to understand Nanjing, to experience Nanjing.

We hope the reading public will become friends with Nanjing.

INTRODUCTION

Bixie (辟邪)

History hangs heavy in the air of Nanjing. The city's central symbol is a mythological animal called the bixie: leonine head and body, the wings of an eagle on its back, the scales of a dragon along its flanks. This chimera's central mission, it is said, is to protect the city of Nanjing, and at first glance one might think that it has not quite been up to the task. The city has been destroyed countless times as successive empires waxed and waned: its inhabitants slaughtered, its relics looted, its monuments and palaces and towers razed.

But a closer look at the bixie reveals a key to both the past and the present of this city: its head is held high, is raised, in fact, to Heaven, not in supplication but in pride, perhaps even defiance. And after each disaster that has befallen this region—the violence and chaos of the aptly named Warring States Period twenty-four hundred years ago; the floods, fires and epidemics of the first thirty years of the Liang dynasty; the death of half the

population at the hands of the warlord Hou Jing in 548 A.D., and the total devastation wrought by the Sui hordes only forty years later; the assault on the city by the Prince of Beijing in his quest to usurp the Ming throne; the bloodstained twelve years overseen by the less aptly named Kingdom of Heavenly Peace; and the unspeakable horror of the Japanese occupation in 1937—the city of Nanjing has risen from the ashes.

南京

This cycle of destruction and rebuilding has transformed present-day Nanjing into a city of matchless cultural and historical depth. Each successive culture has left traces of its passing, from shards of human bone half a million years old, to bronze and ceramic artifacts dating back two millennia, to the remaining monuments of the nations that made Nanjing central to their empires: the Kingdom of Yue and the Eastern Wu, the Eastern Jin, the four kingdoms known collectively as the Southern Dynasties, the Southern Tang, the Ming and Taiping, and lastly the Republic of China.

Chaotian Palace (朝天宫)

In places this historical depth is to be understood literally. The Chaotian Palace, for example, is built on the foundations of an ancient temple raised by the Eastern Jin. It was destroyed and reconstructed several times, and under the Ming became both a center for ancestor worship and a school of court etiquette. The entire complex, including the Confucian temple at its center, was rebuilt by the Qing in the late nineteenth century, and is now a museum specializing in artifacts from the Southern Dynasties period that followed the Eastern Jin.

Among countless other historical remnants, Nanjing is home to one of the world's great engineering failures, a classic example of imperial hubris: the Yangshan Memorial Stele, which was designed by the third Ming emperor on such an unthinkably large scale that it simply couldn't be moved; according to legend, even the gods themselves despaired, and reneged on their promise to help bear the monstrous tablet to its intended place of prominence at the peak of Purple Mountain. However, in a striking example of the many paradoxes that reign here, Nanjing is also the location of the first and perhaps the most significant engineering triumph of the People's Republic of China: the First Nanjing Bridge.

This bridge's immediate purpose was and is to span the Yangtze River; before its construction, trains had to be ferried across the water one carriage at a time. However, given the river's vast width (not to mention the speed and depth and turbulence of its waters, the variation in flow produced by spring snowmelt and summer rains, the structural challenges posed by estuarial bore and tidal pull, and the astounding volume of silt that the river brings from the highlands), this bridge was considered an impossible project by most of the world's great engineers of the time. It was built nonetheless, and now stands as both a logistical triumph and a complex symbol denoting China's coming of age in the modern world.

Focal to the symbolic nature of the bridge is its greater purpose: in connecting two riverbanks, it also connects Beijing to Shanghai, and in so doing conjoins the two latitudinal halves of this vast country. And this is another of Nanjing's central roles: centrality itself. The northern and southern halves of China have always been both defined and divided by the Yangtze River: in the words of Simon Winchester, above the river "are the brain and the heart and soul of China, (the) tall, pale-skinned, wheat-eating, Mandarin-speaking, reclusive and conservative peoples who are true heirs to the Middle Kingdom's five thousand years of uninterrupted history. Below the (river) are the country's muscles and sinews: the stocky, darker, more flamboyant, rice-eating peoples who speak in the furiously complicated coastal dialects, the men and women whose energies and acumen and cunning—and cooking—have spread the goods and words of China to the world beyond."

By virtue of its position on the bank of the Yangtze, Nanjing connects and moderates between north and south. The city is thus far more than simply the sum of its historical records, however triumphant or tragic they might be: the will to rebuild is manifest not only in the successive recoveries of its past, but also in the city as it stands today. It is for its present-day achievements in industry and technology, in higher education and research, in art and artisanship and quality of life, as much as for its historical achievements, that Nanjing has earned its place as a singular destination for visitors from other parts of China, and from abroad.

GEOGRAPHICAL DETERMINANTS

Joseph Brodsky wasn't speaking of Nanjing when he wrote, "There are places where history is inescapable, like a highway accident—places where geography provokes history." But he might as well have been. The geographical features of this area have invariably been a principal determinant of what was built, and when; of how the city was entered and exited and lived in; of who won and who lost in the great game of empire.

There are four main elements that give shape and structure to Nanjing. Two of them are as old as the planet itself: the Yangtze River, which by a quirk of topography here delimits the city to the west and northwest; and Purple Mountain, which towers over it to the east. The other two elements began as natural structures, and later were altered by human hands: the Qinhuai River, whose course was changed not to benefit Nanjing but to harm it; and the city wall, which began as a simple stone bluff on the west side of present-day Nanjing.

Nanjing on the Map
(南京地图)

THE YANGTZE RIVER
长江

Of these four elements, the Yangtze River is in many ways the most important, as without it Nanjing would never have earned the importance it has assumed at various points in Chinese history. The Yangtze takes in the waters of some seven hundred tributaries, and is more than six thousand kilometers long. It runs from Tibet in the west to the East China Sea, depositing Himalayan silt onto the delta outside Shanghai, making China's territory a tiny bit larger (and, on average, a tiny bit shorter) each day.

It was downstream from the imperial shipyards of Nanjing that the great fleets of Zheng He sailed in the fourteenth century on their way to discover the world; five hundred years later, from upstream came the fleets of Hong Xiuquan and his Heavenly Kingdom troops, hoping to forge a pure new world of their own. From downstream came the British gunboats determined to force open the port cities of the Qing, and from upstream now come tour boats loaded with foreigners still awestruck by the Three Gorges hundreds of kilometers away.

Yangtze River
江
長

PURPLE MOUNTAIN
紫金山

Purple Mountain looms always above the skyline to the east of Nanjing, and is the location of many of the city's historical monuments and moments. While several of those sites will be discussed in greater detail elsewhere in this book, a number of them are worth mentioning here.

At the top of the western slope is the Purple Mountain Observatory, a cluster of domed telescopes and modern research facilities that also houses a fine collection of ancient astronomical instruments. South of the observatory is the Botanical Garden, a beautiful space containing more than three thousand species of medicinal and decorative plants, and a fine statue of Li Shizhen, the father of Chinese botany and traditional medicine.

Farther east, on one side of the central ridge is the tomb of Hongwu, the first Ming emperor, with its Sacred Avenue, its pavilions and courtyards, and the immense, as-yet unexcavated burial mound where the emperor's body is believed to lie. Still farther east, at the center of the mountain stands what has become a site of pilgrimage for many local and overseas Chinese: the Sun Yat-Sen Mausoleum. A vast stone stairway leads up to his crypt and his coffin.

李时珍
Li Shizhen

As the high ground closest to the city, Purple Mountain has served alternately in the strategic interests of those who wished to defend the city, and of those who wished to attack it. A burial site here has long been the highest honor the city has to offer to those whose personal history has intersected with its own.

THE QINHUAI RIVER
秦淮河

If one wished to consider the Yangtze as the ego of Nanjing, and the city wall as its superego, there is only one element that could be called its id: the Qinhuai River. While its source lies more than one hundred kilometers away, it is the section that passes through Nanjing which is the most significant, as for centuries it was here that the women of the flower boats were found.

The river had long since been famous as a trading center, first developed during the Southern Dynasties period that preceded the arrival of the Sui, and once the city recovered from the disaster wrought by Emperor Wendi, the riverbank properties, including the flower boats, grew ever more lucrative. For a price, one could choose songs for the women to sing as old men poled the boats downstream; for a significantly higher price, the old men could be left on the bank.

（秦淮画舫）

Eight Beauties of Qinhuai(秦淮八艳)

It should be noted that many of these women were highly cultured, skilled in the classical arts of calligraphy and painting, of singing and dancing, even of chess, and in the best of cases it was these skills that attracted their customers. While this of course does nothing to mitigate the fundamental sadness and exploitation under which most of the women labored, it does somewhat complicate the image of the flower boats as little more than floating brothels.

According to Ye Zhaoyan's *Old Nanjing: Reflections of Scenes on the Qinhuai River*, after wilting under the strictures of the Taiping, the flower boats flourished again for a time in the late Qing, but in the years of the Republic, growing pollution and heavy construction led the women to move from the banks of the river to the "song-and-tea houses" located in and around Gongyuan Street. Such was the situation in 1949 when the Communist armies took Nanjing, and did their best to stamp out the industry altogether.

It must also be said that the Qinhuai has not always been the city's erotic core; it was once simply a river known as Huaishui, and its current course has little in common with its original one. Beginning in 221 B.C., Qin Shihuang united most of present-day China under the banner of his Xian-based Qin empire. Brilliant and ruthless, he is credited with a number of extraordinary achievements: he began construction on what would one day be the Great Wall, and oversaw both the introduction of an efficient weights and measurement system and the standardization of written Chinese; to this day his place in history is defended by the extraordinary army of terracotta warriors

discovered in one section of his mausoleum. Unfortunately, he was also somewhat paranoid, and became obsessed with the notion that somewhere in his vast holdings there were corners with such impeccable feng shui that other leaders would invariably rise there to challenge him. In the course of his imperial surveys, he searched for such corners, and found one here in Nanjing. He brought in hundreds of thousands of workers and ordered them quite literally to move mountains—Fangshan in particular—to destroy the area's topographico-spiritual balance.

Qinhuai River（秦淮河）

Qinhuai River（秦淮河）

Fan Li

范蠡

The riverbanks are now lined primarily with restaurants, apartment buildings and hotels, many of them in buildings reconstructed along their original Qing lines. The flower boats are nowhere to be seen; in their place are tour boats, which depart from the dock in front of the Confucius Temple, head east to the sluice gate at Dongshuimen, then make their way down to the immense citadel at Zhonghuamen. A few landscaped gardens have been added to complement the imported sycamores that have shaded the river for centuries. But beginning in 1996, the city put a great deal of effort and money—about 375 million dollars—into cleaning up the water. As a result, a river that once was black with pollution, more sewer than tourist attraction, is now a pleasant urban waterway.

Outside the city walls, the river can be visited via boats that leave from Stone City Harbor. The riverbanks here, now lined with willows and oleander, were first settled some 2500 years ago. In one place the barest remains of Yue City can be seen on the west bank; there's a rectangular stone foundation that still stands intact and solid at the waterline. There is also a bronze statue of Fan Li, the Yue general who oversaw the city's construction.

Qinhuai River（秦淮河）

THE NANJING CITY WALL
南京古城墙

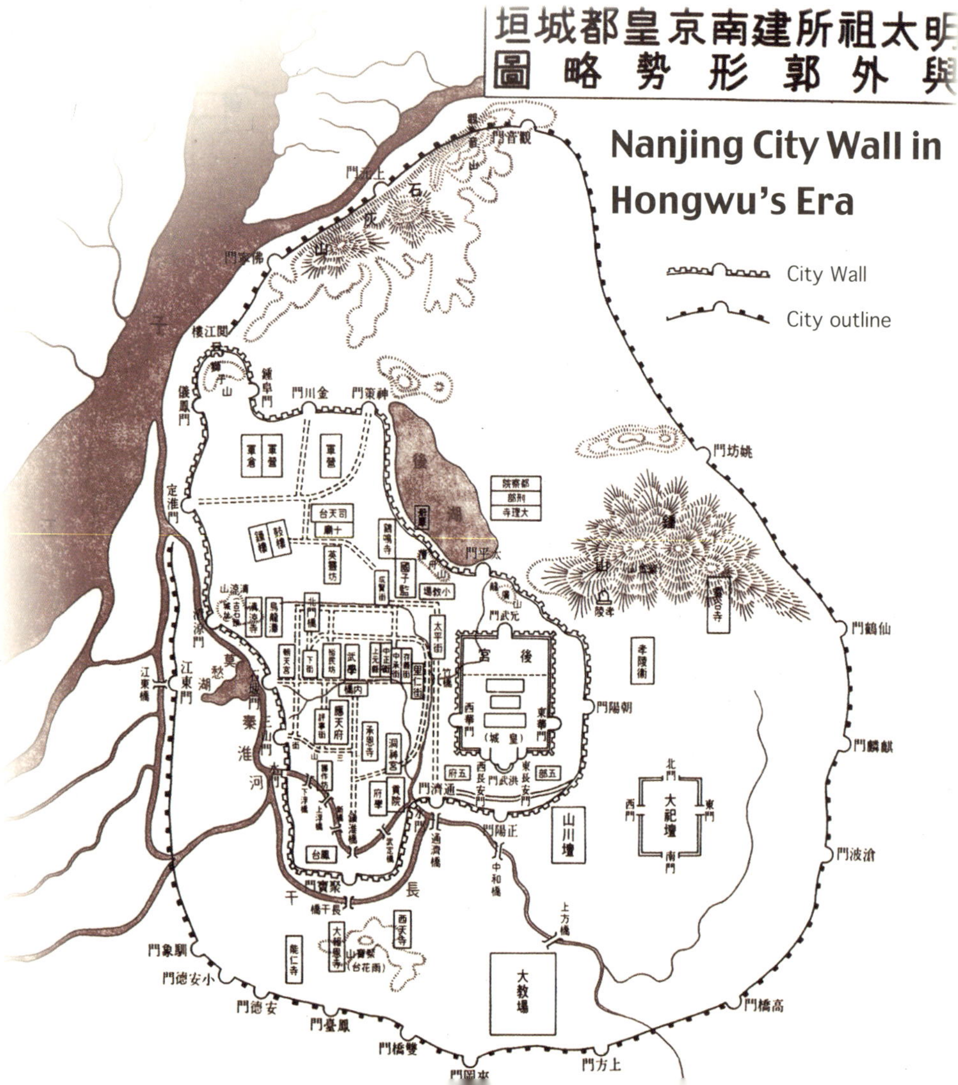

Nanjing City Wall in Hongwu's Era

The origins of the Nanjing city wall stretch back to the third century A.D., when an Eastern Han commander by the name of Sun Quan, who would one day found the Eastern Wu dynasty, ordered the building of Stone City, a wall approximately ten kilometers in length around a citadel at the top of what is now called Qingliang Hill. In fact, nature had already done a good deal of the work: Sun's builders used the immense stony hillside above the river as a starting point, shaved the flanks of the hill where necessary, and filled in the gaps with smaller stones.

Some six hundred years later, the Southern Tang took Nanjing as their capital, rebuilt the city, and extended the wall. The current southern wall follows the same line now as it did then; the Tang wall to the east no longer exists as such, but according to Kerk Phillips' essay "A Concise History of the City of Nanjing: How it Relates to the City You See Today," it can still be made out on contemporary maps of Nanjing, given that the moat which edged that wall has become modern urban streams.

However, the great majority of the wall as it exists today was the work of the first Ming emperor. Hongwu gathered 200,000 laborers, and in the course of the twenty-one years between 1366 and 1386, he supervised its construction. While it is true that the Ming wall incorporates a great deal of what had been built by the Southern Tang, the square form of the older wall was abandoned for a line that snakes its way around the city, taking greater advantage of strategic heights at various locations.

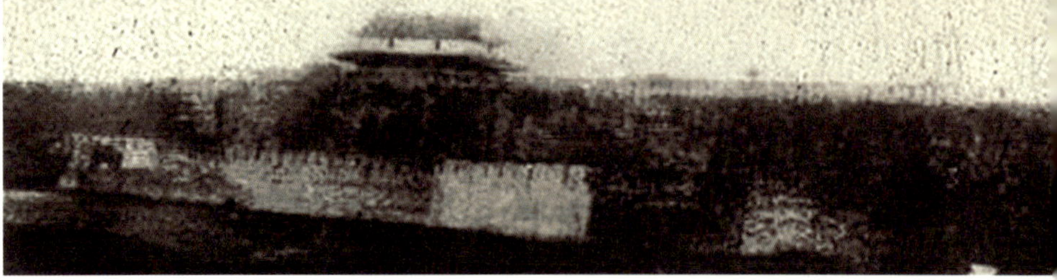

Many of the original city gates, particularly those destroyed during the Japanese invasion, have been wholly or partially rebuilt. Yifengmen was recently reconstructed, and it is now possible to walk on or along the wall from Lion Hill in the northwest to Mochou Lake in the southwest. Another fine walk is along the section that runs west from Jiuhuashan Park at the south end of Xuanwu Lake toward Jiming Temple and Taipingmen. The view across the water and out to the west face of Purple Mountain is spectacular when the weather is clear. Likewise, Dongshuiguan, the east sluice gate, has now been rebuilt; there is perhaps nowhere better for a look down at the sun reflected off the quiet waters of the Qinhuai.

HISTORICAL FEATURES

General Chronology

Dynasty	Sub-dynasty		Reign
Pre-History（史前）			
Xia（夏）			22nd century–17th century BC
Shang（商）			17th century–11th century BC
Zhou（周）	Western Zhou（西周）		11th century–771 BC
	Eastern Zhou（东周）		770–256 BC
Spring-Autumn Period（春秋）			772–481 BC
Warring States Period（战国）			475–211 BC
Qin（秦）			221–206 BC
Han（汉）	Western Han（西汉）		206 BC–25 AD
	Eastern Han（东汉）		25 AD–220 AD
Three Kingdoms（三国）	Wei（魏）		220–265
	Shu（蜀）		221–263
	Wu（吴）		222–280
The Jin（晋）	Western Jin（西晋）		265–420
	Eastern Jin（东晋）		317–420
The Six Dynaties（六朝）	The Southern Dynasties（商朝）	Song（宋）	420–479
		Qi（齐）	479–502
		Liang（梁）	502–557

The Six Dynasties（六朝）	The Southern Dynasties（商朝）	Chen（陈）	557–588
	The Northern Dynasties（北朝）	Northern Wei（北魏）	386–534
		Eastern Wei（东魏）	534–550
		Northern Qi（北齐）	550–577
		Western Wei（西魏）	535–556
		Northern Zhou（北周）	557–581
Sui（隋）			581–618
Tang（唐）			618–907
Five Dynasties and Ten Kingdoms（五代十国）	Later Liang（后梁）		907–923
	Later Tang（后唐）		923–936
	Later Jin（后晋 ）		936–947
	Later Han（后汉）		947–950
	Later Zhou（后周）		951–960
	Southern Tang（南唐）		937–976
Song（宋）	Northern Song（北宋）		960–1127
	Southern Song（南宋）		1127–1279
Yuan（元）			1206–1368
Ming（明）			1368–1644
Qing（清）			1616–1911
Republic of China（中华民国）			1912–1949
People's Republic of China（中华人民共和国）			1949–present

PRE-HISTORY 史前

Historical Sites: Leigong Hill（雷公山）

The history of Nanjing began much as humanity itself is imagined to have begun: in a cave. In this case, the cave in question measures more than twenty meters from floor to ceiling. It is located on Leigong Hill, which rises above a quietly beautiful valley twenty-five kilometers to the east of the city.

Archaeological findings indicate that somewhere between 300,000 and half a million years ago, mid-Pleistocene communities were already forming in this area. The discovery of the cave—and of the skull of a hominid known here as "Nanjing Ape-man"—occurred in 1993. The cave is well stocked with stalactites, and there is a hole about ten centimeters in diameter in the roof through which light pours: the moment of discovery, a miner from nearby Yangshan Quarry expecting to hit rock and instead swinging his pick through the crust into empty air.

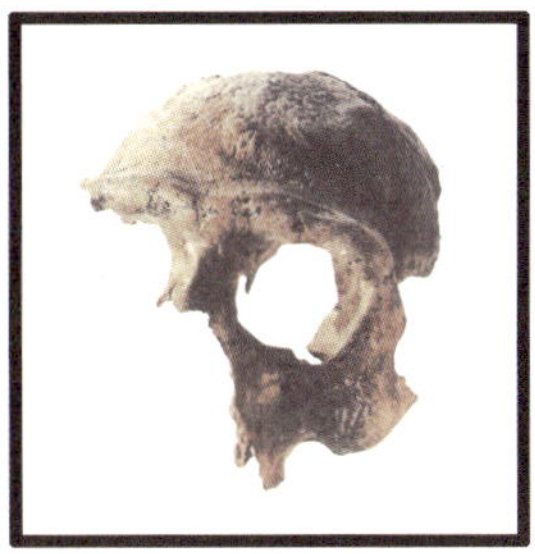

The cave's current iteration—concrete "boulders," colored lights and plaster dioramas, imitation fossils housed in glass boxes that are nearly opaque given the condensation inside—is less than tasteful. The skull itself is kept in a vault in Chaotian Palace and cannot be seen, but there is a reasonably detailed display about the discovery at the Nanjing Museum of Paleontology.

THE BEIYINYANG, THE LIANGZHU, THE SHANG AND THE ZHOU

北阴阳，良渚，商周

3500–771 B.C.

The descendants of those who lived in the Leigong caves began coalescing into the primitive plains villages of the Beiyinyang culture approximately 5500 years ago. Several excavations have unearthed a large number of burial sites containing rudimentary ceramics, tools and jewelry.

Moving forward nearly three millennia, some two hundred sites pertaining to the late Shang and early Zhou dynasties have also been discovered. More advanced agricultural implements and ceramic wares were found at these locations, as were a fair number of bronze artifacts including knives and fishhooks.

Jade, too, bears mentioning here. The Liangzhu culture, which survived for more than a millennium before being absorbed into the Shang dynasty, possessed a sphere of influence extending from Nanjing to Shanghai, including Lake Tai and what is now the city of Hangzhou. An extraordinary cache of jade artifacts was discovered at the Third Tomb of Sidun, dating to approximately 2500 B.C. Much of the jade is in the form of ceremonial pieces such as bi (a circular ring used in ceremonies honoring heaven), and cong (a long square tube used in ceremonies honoring the earth). According to Jerrod Roalstad of the University of Minnesota, some of these pieces bear the earliest known examples of the taotie, a zoomorphic mask design showing what is most often (though not universally) considered to be a full dragon face split at the center of the nose to form two separate dragons in face-to-face confrontation. A number of researchers have posited that the Liangzhu would have needed magnifying glasses of some sort, and perhaps diamond-tipped awls, to create these elaborate carvings.

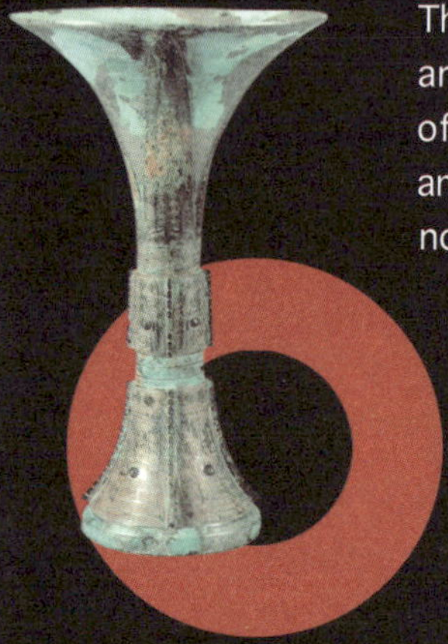

The importance of jade to this area is not simply a matter of pretty trinkets worn by and buried with the local elite, nor of objects of religious or symbolic importance, however great. In fact, the discoveries of Liangzhu jade have contributed greatly to a reevaluation of the entire history of China. According to the historians of the National Gallery of Art in Washington D.C., "Until this century, China's remote past was known mainly from historical narratives written during the Han dynasty (206 B.C.-A.D. 220). References to the prehistoric period in these texts are few, however, and include vague claims, such as the existence of a 'jade age', which modern scholars considered the stuff of legend. The advent of archaeology has provided a means to distinguish fact from fiction. (...) The most significant result is a new view of the origin of Chinese civilization, which was long believed to have arisen in the Yellow River valley and spread from there throughout the country. Excavations over the past few decades have revealed that prehistoric societies also flourished along the Yangtze River to the south (...), demonstrating

that Chinese civilization developed not from a single source, but through the gradual blending of several distinct cultures."

Artifacts

Many spectacular examples of Liangzhu jade are on display at the Jiangsu Provincial Museum in Nanjing, including a beautiful curved xi with a human face clearly visible on its convex side. The museum also has some fine examples of Xia-era lacquer ware, which was invented approximately seven thousand years ago here in Jiangsu province, and of bronze wine vessels from the Shang and Zhou dynasties. Finally, they have an excellent collection of painted ceramics from local cultures dating back to 5000 B.C., including the Qingliangang, North Yinyangying, and Dawengkou cultures. The work of this last group is perhaps the most interesting, as they invented techniques for applying compound colors in complex patterns often taken from floral and weaving motifs.

THE SPRING AND AUTUMN PERIOD, THE WARRING STATES PERIOD, THE QIN, AND THE HAN

春秋，战国，秦汉

770 B.C. – 220 A.D.

Key Historical Figures: **Fu Chai** (夫差)
Goujian (勾践)
Qin Shihuang (秦始皇)

Nanjing's Many Names

南京城市名称变更记

The End of the Spring and Autumn 春秋未期	Ye Cheng（冶城）（770–475B.C.） Yue Cheng（越城）（472B.C.）
The Warring States 战国	Jin Ling Cheng（金陵城）（333B.C.）
The Qin and the Han 秦汉	Mo Ling（秣陵）
The Three Kingdoms 三国	Jian Ye（建邺）(229B.C.)
The Jin 晋	Jian Kang（建康）(317)
The Ming 明	Ying Tianfu（应天府） Nanjing（南京）
The Qin 清	Jiang Ning（江宁）
The Republic and the Warlords 民国	Nanjing（南京）(1911B.C.)

While it is true that there is little in the way of reliable written historical records prior to the establishment of the Han dynasty, certain earlier periods have left us enough evidence to piece together a historical framework for the Nanjing area.

Toward the end of the Spring and Autumn Period (770-475 B.C.), Prince Fu Chai of the Wu Kingdom built a center for metalwork primarily focused on making swords for his soldiers. The main foundry, known as Yecheng (Metallurgical City), is believed to have been established in 495 B.C., and was located on Yeshan Hill near what later became the Chaotian Palace.

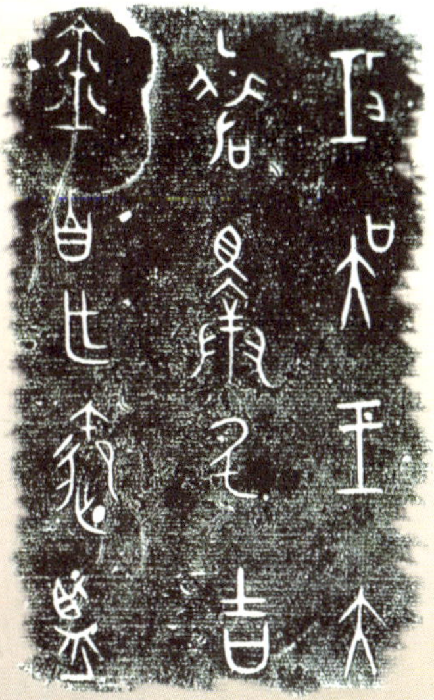

For much of the next three hundred fifty years, Nanjing suffered along with the rest of China during the Warring States Period (476-22 B.C.), with two nearby kingdoms, the Yue and the Chu, fighting the Wu for control of the area. In 472 B.C., the Yue king, Goujian, led his troops to victory, and built a small fortified city named Yue City just south of present-day Nanjing. A century and a half later, it was the turn of the Chu, who vanquished the Yue and built a town known as Jinling (Gold Hill), in the area on and around Qingliang Hill; this is the first manifestation of Nanjing in its current location.

Following Qin Shihuang's rearrangement of the surrounding topography in the late third century B.C., the city became known as Moling (Hay Hill). The area then enjoyed a long period of relative stability, as Moling served as the administrative center for the surrounding region. And for once the city retained its name through a series of dynasties, up to and including that of the Eastern Han in the year 25 A.D.

Artifacts

Again, the best place to see artifacts from these eras is the Jiangsu Provincial Museum. From the Spring and Autumn Era there are some lovely bronze bells, water vessels with dragon and fish-scale motifs, and a beautiful jade sword handle. From the Warring States period, among the finest bronzes are a tall wine vessel topped with a singing bird, another with a gold stopper in the form of a crouching leopard, a reclining deer whose body is inlaid with turquoise, and a beautiful reticulated bronze pot; there is also a fine jade cong with a silver base, and a pair of extraordinary belt-hooks, one of gold and one of gilded silver. And from the Eastern Han there is a terrific array of artifacts, including a bronze ox-shaped lamp with inlays of gold and silver, gold ornaments in the shape of dragons and pyramids, and a terracotta horse that has been adopted as the symbol of tourism in Nanjing. (Harried travelers will find this particularly appropriate, given that the horse's expression changes from ecstatically happy to plainly psychotic depending on the angle from which it is viewed.) However, perhaps the finest piece from the Eastern Han is a death shroud. Discovered in 1970 in a tomb at Tushan, it includes a hood, a face cover, a full coat, gloves, trousers and shoes, all made of small pieces of green jade sewn together with silver wire. In all the suit consists of more than 2600 separate pieces of jade and nearly two pounds of silver.

THE THREE KINGDOMS

三国 220–280A.D.

Emperor: Sun Quan (孙权)

Liu Bei (刘备)

Cao Cao (曹操)

Historical Sites: Stone City（石头城）

Sun's Tomb（孙权墓）

孙权
Sun Quan

Throughout the seven-hundred-year period from the Wu to the Han, Nanjing carried little political weight. However, during the Three Kingdoms period that followed, the city acquired a new and far greater importance. Sun Quan named himself king of the Eastern Wu dynasty in 221 A.D., and eight years later he moved his court here to Nanjing. The Eastern Wu capital, whose name he changed from Moling to Jianye, was located mainly between the Qinhuai and Xuanwu Lake. His three-decade reign was a time of growing prosperity and progress, thanks in no small part to his success in increasing foreign trade and addressing the region's irrigation needs.

Sun Quan 孙权

While there is little of the Eastern Wu left within the city, Sun Quan did leave behind two noteworthy sites. First, as mentioned previously, Stone City, the first manifestation of the Nanjing wall, can still be visited. Second, his tomb is located not far from the city, on a part of Purple Mountain known as Plum Blossom Hill, just south of the far more prominent tomb of Hongwu, the first Ming emperor.

There is some debate as to why Sun's tomb was allowed to remain in place so close to that of Hongwu. One story, perhaps apocryphal, holds that when the suggestion was made to Hongwu that Sun be moved, the Ming emperor agreed that the temple built over Sun's tomb could be relocated, but said that the tomb itself should stay where it was, so that the Eastern Wu king could serve as his janitor. Another story holds that geomantic studies were carried out, and it was determined that the position of Sun's tomb was actually favorable

to the Ming ruler's chances in the afterlife. However it came to be spared, the hill where Sun's tomb is located is particularly noteworthy for its gardens, which contain 15,000 plum trees of two hundred thirty different varieties.

Artifacts

Relatively few artifacts remain from the Three Kingdoms period, but some miniature clay animals, tiny models of entire temples, and ceramic tiles and pots can be seen at the museum in Chaotian Palace. The Jiangsu Provincial Museum also has a few nice pieces, including a beautiful bronze lamp in the shape of a short-armed Immortal riding a lithe bixie.

THE JIN
晋 265–420 A.D.

Map of Jin Sites
晋代历史景点图

Key Historical Figures: **Wang Dao** (王导)
Xie An (谢安)

Historical Sites: **Wang-Xie Residence** (王谢故居)
Cock-crow Temple (鸡鸣寺)

In 317 A.D., the Jin capital of Luoyang was destroyed by the Xiongnu tribes from the north. One of the deceased emperor's sons had been serving as governor of the Nanjing area for almost a decade at that point, and he promptly named himself emperor of a new dynasty called the Eastern Jin.

Though the Eastern Jin emperors were not a particularly strong lot, conditions elsewhere in China were far worse, and Nanjing (then known as Jiankang) grew steadily in wealth and influence. Skilled technicians expanded the textile and ceramics industries, and metalworking reached new heights. Nanjing continued to increase in wealth, fame and population—at its height as the Eastern Jin capital, the city had well over a million inhabitants—until the beginning of the sixth century.

Wang-Xie Residence

(王谢故居)

A fair number of sites have survived from this period. One is the Wang-Xie Residence, which stands near the Confucius Temple in the southern part of the city. It is located on Wuyi Xiang (Black Clothes Lane), a name which hearkens back even further, to the black uniforms worn by Eastern Wu soldiers who once stood guard here.

Wang Dao was a Jin government minister from a family line famous for its achievements in the arts. They lived here for decades, but when they moved elsewhere in Nanjing, the house became the residence of Xie An, also a government minister, though his ancestors were better known for their achievements on the battlefield.

The house was then immortalized by the Tang poet Liu Yuxi who was, as it happens, a descendant of the Wang family. One of Liu's poems laments the loss of aristocratic privilege and refinery—and the subsequent entrance of "barbarians" into Nanjing's public life—with the line, "Gone are the swallows from the Wang-Xie Mansion, into the houses of the common."

The house itself has been preserved mainly because of that line; it can still be visited, but there isn't a great deal to see. One point of interest is what looks to be a small maze carved into the stone of the floor: this is in fact a small-scale model of a certain winding

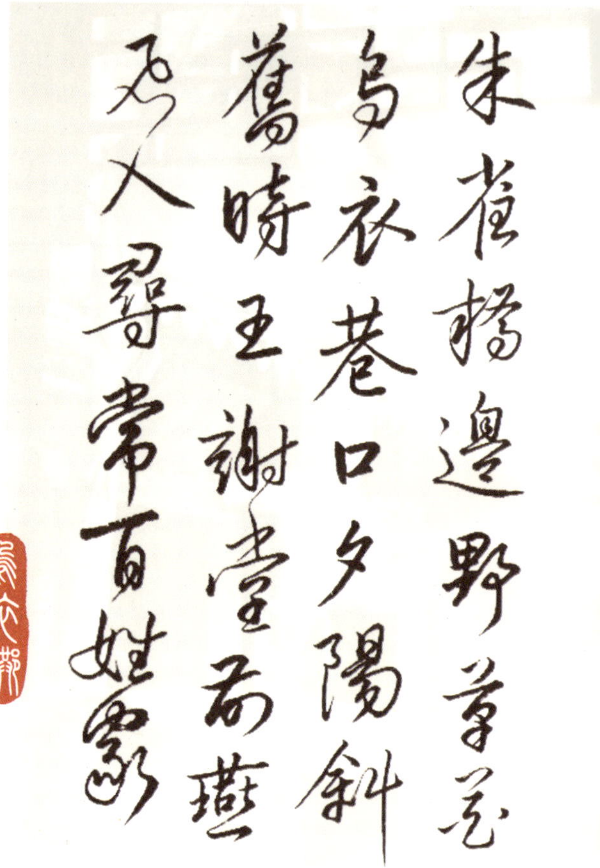

creek located in a bamboo forest in nearby Zhejiang Province. This creek was the refuge of seven famous Jin scholars, who went there as often as possible to compose poetry and enjoy one another's company; other motives for their repeated trips included avoiding what they saw as the more vulgar aspects of society, and distancing themselves from the deadly political intrigues that were commonplace in the life of the imperial court.

The scholars would station themselves at various points along the bank, and float a bowl of wine down the stream. Whichever scholar happened to be seated closest to the point where the bowl first touched land had to drink it dry and then compose a poem. One of those scholars, a man by the name of Ji Kai, was later executed by the Jin emperor for refusing a point-blank invitation to become a court advisor. Another managed to escape the same fate only by maintaining himself in a state of perpetual inebriation, such that the invitation was never extended.

Cock-crow Temple

(鸡鸣寺)

While these poets kept themselves busy with sylvan recitals, several thousand monks were working rather harder in the interest of spreading a new religion throughout China. Buddhism had only recently arrived from its birthplace in India, and many of the temples built over the course of the next few hundred years are very much worth a visit.

Jiming Si (Cock-crow Temple) is located on a hill in the northeast part of the city. It is an extraordinary location, and each edifice is built successively higher on the hill, as if the temple itself were climbing toward the sky. Most of the buildings are bright yellow, with dark red trim and beautiful tile roofs. The view east looks past the city wall and across Xuanwu Lake to the foothills of Purple Mountain.

The temple was founded at the beginning of the Jin dynasty, though most of the buildings now in use were built by the Ming. During the Liang dynasty (502-556 A.D.) it was known as the Tongtai Temple; in the year 527, the first Liang emperor sequestered himself here, and refused to return to the throne until his own government had paid a sizable "ransom." This happened a total of four times here and elsewhere, and was either simply a means of subsidizing his favorite monasteries, or a desperate gesture that he hoped would lead Heaven to cease tormenting his reign with natural and other disasters.

Jiming itself was the most important temple in Nanjing throughout the ensuing Southern Dynasties period, which is saying a great deal, as by then there were some four hundred eighty temples in the area. Under the Southern Tang it was renamed Jing Ju, and then Yuan Ji. The Song called it Fabao Temple, and its current name was finally bestowed in the year 1387, a gift from Ming emperor Hongwu.

Near the middle of the hill is the Buddha Mercy Hall, with its statue of the 1000-hand Buddha. Still lower is the Bhaisajyaguru Pagoda; recently rebuilt, it stands nearly forty-five meters high, with a bucket arch and several layers of eaves. Bhaisajyaguru translates as Buddha of Medicine or Healing Buddha, and on the ground floor there is a Ming-era bronze image of him which rises seven meters high. On the second floor there are four smaller gold images of him in hand-carved niches, also from the Ming.

Artifacts

The Chaotian Palace museum holds several artifacts from the Jin: there are dozens of jade pieces, and a fascinating ceramic night pot in the shape of a lion, with the sole opening being that of the lion's maw. There is also a beautiful glass box, and a display of funerary tablets and epitaph scenes carved in relief. Meanwhile, at the Jiangsu Provincial Museum there are several beautiful gold pieces, including an exquisite thimble and an intricate, stylized ornament in the shape of an Immortal riding a dragon through the clouds.

THE SOUTHERN DYNASTIES
南唐 420–588 A.D.

Nanjing's Location during the Six Dynasties, the Southern Dynasties and the Ming Dynasties (南京六朝，南唐，明代沿革图)

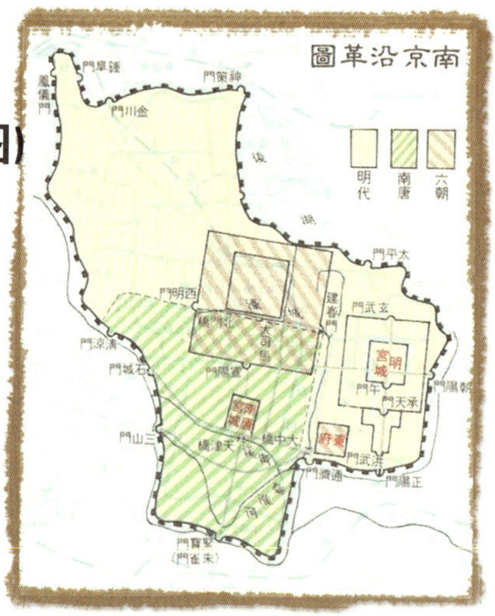

Key Historical Figures: **Liu Yu** (刘裕)

Yun Guang (云光)

Qiu Nu (秋妞)

Historical Sites: **Linggu Temple** (灵谷寺)

Beamless Hall (无梁殿)

Rain Flower Pavilion (雨花台)

Qixia Temple (栖霞寺)

Mochou Lake (莫愁湖)

Map of Southern Dynasties Sites
(南唐历史景点图)

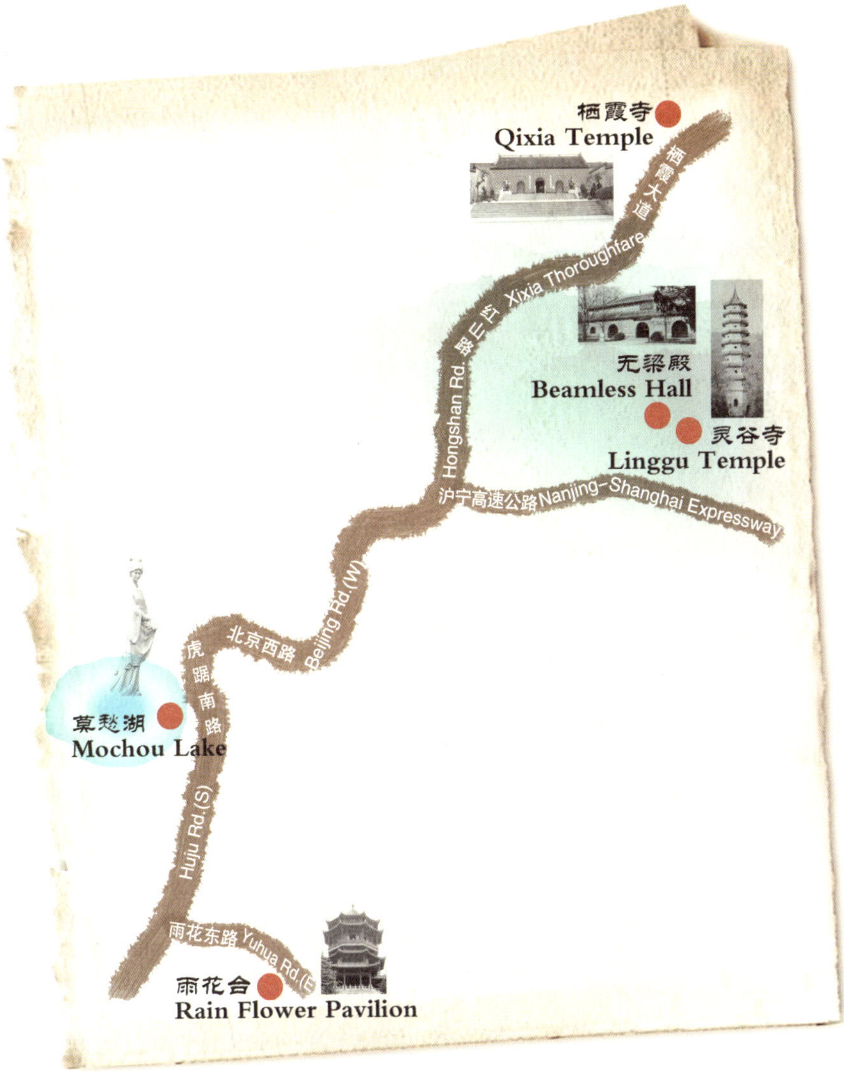

The Eastern Jin dynasty was followed by a period in which four short-lived kingdoms held sequential control: the Song (420-478; often referred to as the Liu Song to distinguish it from the Song empire of the tenth to the thirteenth centuries), the Qi (479-501), the Liang (502-556), and the Chen (557-588).

This is an exceedingly complex period in Chinese history, from the moment a brilliant Eastern Jin general named Liu Yu tired of the antics of his emperor and founded his own dynasty, straight through to the ignominious death of the last Chen king at the hands of the Sui. It was a time of constant political strife, of plots and counterplots, with each of the first three dynasties finally succumbing not to any foreign power but to internal chaos and corruption. However, as northern China had long since been plunged into violent chaos by a series of nomadic tribes, skilled craftsmen and artists continued to migrate south. By the mid-sixth century, no city in China could match Nanjing in terms of cultural and economic strength. As a result, many of the sites most worth visiting were founded in this period.

For further information on the dynastic twists and turns of this era, and on the many tomb carvings and other statuary that the Southern Dynasties left scattered through the fields and villages around Nanjing, Barry Till's *In Search of Old Nanjing* is an indispensable resource.

Linggu Temple
(灵谷寺)

The Linggu Temple was originally part of a large complex built at the northeast foot of Purple Mountain during the Liang dynasty. It remained there until 1381, when the first Ming Emperor decided to build his own tomb on the site. But instead of being destroyed, the temple (along with nearby Beamless Hall) was taken to pieces, and then rebuilt a few kilometers to the east. This compromise allegedly occurred to the temple's head abbot, Bao Zhi, as he lay on his deathbed. His own grave suffered a rather worse fate; the exact site of his re-burial is no longer known. Perhaps in compensation, both Zhigong Hall (built in 1934) and the Baogong Stupa (built in 1941) are now dedicated to the abbot's memory.

In its "new" location, the temple (which was destroyed in the mid-nineteenth century during the Taiping Rebellion, and reconstructed by Qing architect Zeng Guofan in 1867) holds several statues of the Goddess of Mercy, and has a display dedicated to Xuan Zang, the seventh-century Tang monk who brought six hundred fifty original Buddhist scriptures from India to China for translation. (The display includes a model of a 13-story pagoda which holds what is said to be part of Xuan's skull.) His nineteen-year, round-trip voyage involved countless hardships, and upon his return he was feted by the Tang emperor. That odyssey gave rise to a vast number of folk tales and plays, as well as the classic novel *Journey to the West* by the sixteenth-century author Wu Cheng'en.

Beamless Hall

(无梁殿)

Wuliang Dian (Beamless Hall) is true to its name: all masonry, no wood, no supporting beams of any kind. It has a beautiful vaulted ceiling, and there is a large stone platform where the shrine to the Amitabha Buddha once stood. The building's purpose is no longer religious, however; in 1929 it became the "Sacrificial Hall to Guomindang Officers and Men Fallen in Battle." The names of all 33,224 Nationalist officers and soldiers who perished in the Northern Expedition of 1925-1927 are listed on stone tablets. There are also life-sized models of such men in full battle-gear.

Because there is little light inside—buildings without beams do not lend themselves well to windows—the models are a bit hard to make out. However, in addition to the scenes testifying to battles against the warlords, there are a few other historical moments thrown in: Lin Zhexu burning British opium shipments in 1849; the signing of the humiliating treaty with the British that ended the Second Opium War; and British and French soldiers happily sacking the Summer Palace in Beijing in 1860.

Rain Flower Pavilion (雨花石)

Nearly everywhere one goes in Nanjing, one is approached—at times accosted—by people selling pretty pieces of multi-colored stone. Some of the stones are rough and some are polished; some are cut and some whole; some are genuine agate, and others not so much. The stones invariable sit in small bowls of water, and are truly beautiful. These are the Rain Flower Pebbles.

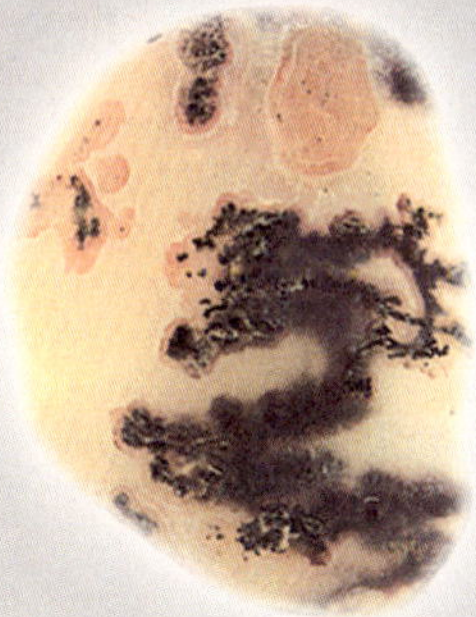

These stones actually have their own museum on the Rain Flower Terrace just south of the city. The information given there is minimal, but the rocks are lovely: crystals, limestone, and a great deal of agate, much of it set in jewelry. On one wall there is a large stone with a naturally occurring stain in the form of Karl Marx; another, oddly, is the spitting image of Margaret Thatcher.

At one point there were enough temples in this area to house and support nearly 10,000 monks. Now only one such building remains, the Rain Flower Pavilion, from the gate of which monks once preached on Buddhist scripture to the gathered crowds. One of those monks was Yun Guang, whose name means "Light from the Clouds," in reference to a beautiful weather phenomenon that occurs here from time to time. According to legend, one morning in the year 507 A.D., the Immortals decided to rain flowers down upon him for preaching so deftly and beautifully. The flowers then turned into the agate now found glowing in bowls of water on every street corner, for sale, like saints' bones, only prettier.

In the center of the pavilion there is a statue of Yun Guang, and around the circular inner wall are images from his life. There's also a mural showing the angel-like beings who sent the flowers downward, and paintings of the temple and grounds as they are imagined to have been at the time.

Qixia Temple (栖霞寺)

Yet another storied temple bears mentioning here: Qixia Temple, named for the red clouds that often appear to perch upon the hill where the temple stands. It is located about twenty kilometers northeast of the city, and was founded in 489 on land donated by a pious recluse named Ming Sengshao. For centuries it has been one of the most important monasteries in the country, though much of it was destroyed by the Taiping and subsequently rebuilt by the Qing.

Passing through the tower at the main gate, one sees another gate, inside of which the Deva Kings stand guard. Beyond this is the main courtyard, with the Vairocana Hall at the far side. This double-eaved hall is immense, and holds a massive statue of the Vairocana Buddha. Behind it are the monks' living quarters, and another hall used for large gatherings.

Out the gate to the east is the Sheli Ta, a white octagonal pagoda originally built during the Sui dynasty at the beginning of the seventh century, and renovated extensively by the Southern Tang. Eight images from the Buddha's life are carved in relief on the base.

毘盧寶殿

From there a stone path heads north up the forested slopes of Qixia Hill, into a vast complex of carved niches containing a total of five hundred thirteen statues of the Buddha, as well as a final niche holding what is said to be a statue of the original mason. The oldest of these statues date back to the Qi; some are larger than life-size, and some are less than thirty centimeters tall. Unfortunately, very few are still intact: many were damaged during the Taiping Rebellion, and others were destroyed during the Cultural Revolution by Red Guards who used the temple as a barracks until 1979.

In many of the niches, the back wall is stained a red that was once dark and now has faded. The higher one climbs on the mountain, the more complete the destruction is: missing heads, missing arms or hands. Early in the twentieth century, the monks attempted to repair some of the statues with cement which is now crumbling.

Mochou Lake (莫愁湖)

河中水之歌

河中之水向东流　洛阳女儿名莫愁

莫愁十三能织绮　十四采桑南陌头

十五嫁为卢家妇　十六生子字阿侯

卢家兰室桂为梁　中有郁金苏合香

头上金钗十二行　足下丝履五文章

珊瑚挂镜难生光　平头奴子擎履箱

人生富贵何所望　恨不早嫁东家王

The final Southern Dynasties site worth visiting is not a temple but a body of water known as Mochou Lake, located southwest of Shuiximen, just outside the city wall. 1500 years ago, the scenery here was said to be the most beautiful in all of Nanjing; the lake is still very pleasant, lined with willows and full of lotus blossoms and water lilies.

In the early years of the Liang dynasty, a merchant from Nanjing took a trip to Henan, and as he passed through a village in Luoyang he saw a young girl crying over the body of her father. The merchant saw that the girl was too poor to bury her father properly, and took pity on her; he gave her money for the burial, then adopted her and brought her to Nanjing.

The girl, Qiu Nu, grew into a beautiful, kind-hearted young woman, and was given the nickname now attributed to the lake itself: Mo Chou, meaning "Carefree" or "Without Sorrow." She later married the merchant's son, and quickly learned how to make silk brocade, which brought her additional accolades. Unfortunately, her beauty and skills attracted the envy of the neighbors, one of whom connived to have her husband sent to a dangerous border post. The neighbor then attempted to rape Mo Chou; to prevent him from doing so, she drowned herself in the lake.

Around the lake are a number of small buildings, including Yujin Hall, which has a portrait of Mo Chou, and the Square Pavilion, which holds a statue of her cut from white Han jade. Also here is the Victorious Chess Pavilion; around the base there is a series of scenes in bas-relief, most of them displaying victory in what look to be very bloody battles. The pavilion was destroyed by the Taiping, then rebuilt in 1871; it contains original Ming furniture made of mahogany, with mother-of-pearl and abalone inlay.

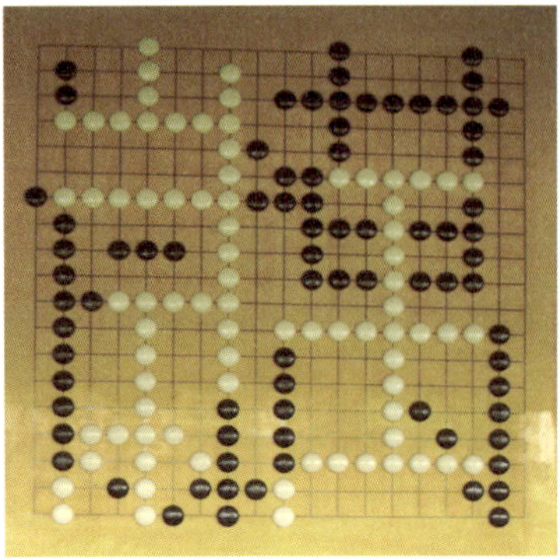

It is said that the first Ming emperor often came to this pavilion to play chess against his top general, Xu Da. In the course of one such match, Hongwu suspected that Xu was losing on purpose so as not to anger him. He instructed Xu to play his best; in the end, the emperor won, and made no attempt to conceal his pride. Then Xu asked him to come around to look at the board from Xu's side. The emperor did so, and saw that Xu had lost very, very carefully, such that the remaining pieces on the board formed the characters signifying "ten thousand years," a tribute equivalent to "Long live the Emperor," and a fine way for Xu to demonstrate his humility and his skill simultaneously.

Artifacts

The Chaotian Palace museum has several interesting artifacts from this period, including a large and handsome bixie, its chest rubbed smooth by the hands of tourists. It also has reproductions of two fascinating vehicles that accompanied the Liang emperors on their longer voyages. One is a two-wheeled open cart with a long tongue carved in the form of a dragon's head; it is called a "compass vehicle," and rising from its center is a tall wooden post, at the top of which stands a magnetized human figure that pivots freely, such that its outstretched arm always points south.

The other vehicle is a primitive odometer, with gears connecting the cart wheels to a wooden carving composed of several pieces: one monk holds a large drum which another monk beats once for each five hundred meters the vehicle traverses.

Among the important pieces from this period in the Jiangsu Provincial Museum are a set of tiny gold animal-shaped ornaments from the Qi, and several jade pieces, including a pale green pei-pendant bearing a dragon on one side and a phoenix on the other. Additionally, there is a terrific collection of pieces made of the yellow-green porcelain known as celadon: there is a beautiful ewer adorned with the head of a sheep, a covered jar with six rings and an overturned lotus design, and a surprisingly delicate spittoon, all from the Southern Dynasties. Finally, there is an entire wall of gray brick bearing an intricate design: an Immortal dancing away from a tiger's bared teeth, the flowers and grass seeming to sway in a breeze one can almost feel.

THE SUI AND THE TANG

隋唐 581–907 A.D.

Key Historical Figures: **Emperor Wendi** (隋文帝)

Li Shiming (李世民)

Xuan Zang (玄藏)

As noted, by the end of the Southern Dynasties period, Nanjing was one of the most prosperous and culturally advanced cities in China. Then came the armies of the first Sui emperor, Wendi. Fearing that the area's prominence would lead to thoughts of resistance to his rule, in 589 A.D. he razed the city, slaughtered its inhabitants, plowed even its foundations into the ground, and turned the whole area into farmland. The Chen emperor was found cowering in a well with several of his concubines. He was promptly dispatched, but his hiding place is now known as the Rouge Well, in honor of the reddish stains alleged to be from either the blood or the make-up of the concubines.

During the subsequent Tang dynasty (618-907), Nanjing gradually recovered. For the next two hundred years it served as an economic center of some importance, before once again coming under the sword in the late tenth century.

Artifacts

While there are few Sui or Tang sites remaining, artifacts from this period can be seen at the Jiangsu Provincial Museum. There is a fascinating set of brightly painted warriors made of clay, their expressions fierce and their poses triumphant. It was also at this time that lacquer ware artisans developed new techniques for using gold, mother-of-pearl and rhino skin as part of the embossed surfaces of their dishes and ornaments, and many of these are worth seeing. Finally, there is a beautiful imperial mandate scroll on display, annotated by three famous Tang calligraphers and marked with their seals.

THE FIVE DYNASTIES AND TEN KINGDOMS

五代十国 907–979 A.D.

Key Historical Figures: Li Bian (李昪)
Li Jing (李璟)

Historical Sites: Tombs of the Southern Tang Emperors（南唐墓）

As the Greater Tang dynasty disintegrated in the early tenth century, China entered a period of regionalization. In 937, Nanjing was rebuilt to serve as the capital of a local dynasty, the Southern Tang, which lasted until 975, outliving its founder by only thirty-two years. As noted, the city wall was also rebuilt, its square base serving as the outline for the much vaster wall later built by the Ming. Zhonghuamen was the city's main south entrance then as now, the wall running north from Tongjimen and then west past what is now the entrance to Nanjing University.

The first Southern Tang emperor also built an inner walled area known as the Zicheng; his palace was inside, though its exact location is no longer clear. Furthermore, he ordered the construction of a summer palace and several temples on Qingliang Hill.

By far the most interesting remains from this period are the tombs of the first two Southern Tang emperors. (The third and final emperor was captured by the Song in 974, and taken to Kaifeng; he was murdered there shortly thereafter.) The tombs are located about fifteen kilometers south of the city, on Zutang Mountain in neighboring Jiangning County, and are a bit of work to get to, but are well worth the effort.

Tombs of the Southern Tang Emperors (南唐墓)

The inner brick walls of both tombs were originally covered with a layer of limestone-based plaster painted with red lacquer. Most of the plaster has crumbled away, but where it remains, much of the original lacquer is still a beautiful dark red; in other places it is streaked with age, and has the appearance of blood marble.

In the tomb of the first emperor, Li Bian, one passes through a

narrow archway into a room with a beautiful vaulted ceiling, and small niches to either side known as "treasure bins." Most of what they contained was taken by the thieves who discovered the tomb in 1949 or 1950, but some jade pieces were later found, as well as some porcelain and a number of clay figures. There are still a few discernible floral designs on the walls and ceiling: reds and blues and yellows in simple patterns.

Through another archway there is a second room, again with niches to east and west; at the far end is the doorway to the innermost room, the tomb itself. Two warriors stand guard to either side of the door. They are carved in relief, round-faced and a little baffled-looking, their hands crossed on the hilts of their swords. Above the door is a beautiful stone carving of two dragons disputing a pearl, the dragons long-tongued and vicious, the gloss on them still high despite the centuries that have passed.

The double-doors themselves are immense slabs of stone more than two meters tall, one and a half meters wide and twenty centimeters thick. Despite their weight, they were originally hung on pairs of hinges; the holes carved in the walls where the hinges attached can still be seen. In each door, there are five horizontal rows of seven small decorative holes; it is said that if the emperor had managed to unite the whole country, there would instead be nine holes in each row.

Sadly, the top center corners of both doors were broken by the tomb raiders. Inside, the emperor's bier can still be seen, but it has likewise been broken, this time by Red Guards. The wood of the coffin has long since disintegrated, but there are two interesting carvings in the stone floor; to the right of the bier is a representation of the Yangtze River, and to the left, one of the Yellow River.

The tomb of the second emperor, Li Jing, is less finely furnished but in somewhat better condition: his bier, at least, is whole, though here too most of the artifacts were stolen. As in his father's tomb, the lighting is minimal, a question of bare light bulbs, but instead of detracting from the medieval feel of the place, this in fact adds to it: bits of mica in the limestone glitter coldly wherever the plaster remains on the walls and ceiling.

The tomb sites are surrounded by a beautiful cypress grove. There is a lake nearby, and a small exhibition room showing reproductions of things found in the tombs—clay figures of sheep and chickens and camels, of family members and servants, of dancers.

Artifacts

Many of the original Southern Tang tomb figures are on permanent display at the Jiangsu Provincial Museum, including a beautiful set of dancers, one male and one female; the Southern Tang rulers often brought musicians and dancers in from other countries, and these two figures are clearly modeled on foreigners, with their deep-set eyes and large noses, not to mention the male figure's thick beard. Also here are the Mourning Books, a set of forty-two gorgeous jade tablets engraved with gold that proclaim the achievements of these two emperors to all with eyes to read.

THE SONG

宋 960-1279A.D.

Map of Song Sites
(宋代历史景点图)

Key Historical Figures: **Tai Zu Zhao Kuangyin** (太祖赵匡胤)

Zhen Zong (真宗)

Shen Zong (神宗)

Wang Anshi (王安石)

Historical Sites: **Imperial Examination Hall** (江南贡院)

Confucius Temple (夫子庙)

In the year 975, the Southern Tang dynasty was brought to an abrupt end by the armies of the Song. However, when the Song imperial capital at Kaifeng fell to thc Tartars in 1126, one of the emperor's sons fled here, and for twelve years Nanjing was again the seat of empire.

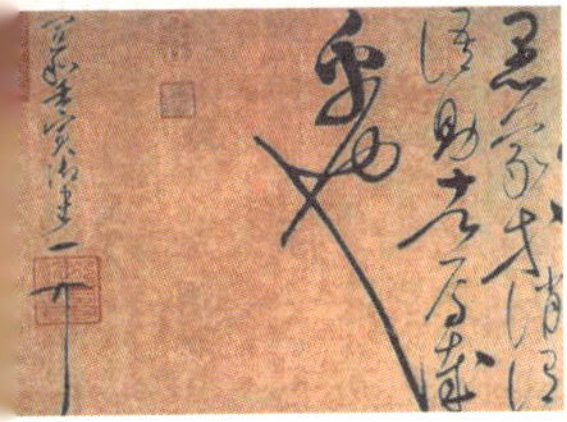

This dynasty, now known as the Southern Song, later moved its capital to Hangzhou; from that moment until the end of the Yuan dynasty more than two hundred years later, the former Southern Tang palace—expanded and improved during the early years of the Southern Song—was used as office space for the local prefecture.

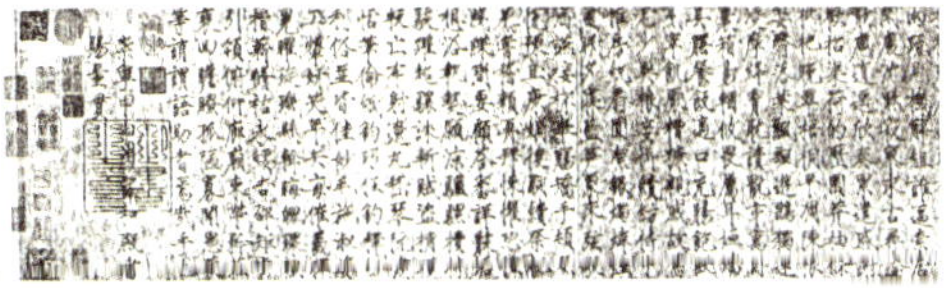

Among the most interesting sites left by the Song is Jiangnan Gongyuan, the Imperial Examination Hall. Built in 1168, at its peak it had a vast number of exam cells—some 20,644 all told, the majority built later under the Ming and Qing, and in certain years even that number wasn't enough to accommodate all the scholars that flooded in from the provinces. The examinees spent nine days writing

(江南贡院) Imperial Examination Hall

essays that demonstrated their knowledge and understanding of Confucian thought. During those nine days, the scholars were not allowed to leave the tiny cells; servants brought food, each cell had a chamber pot, and the writing surface of each desk could be lowered to form a small, uncomfortable bunk.

明經取士　爲國求賢

三人行 必有我师焉 择其善者而从之 择其不善者而改之

Confucius Temple

(夫子庙)

Another site bequeathed to Nanjing by the Southern Song has become one of the city's central landmarks: Fuzi Miao, better known as the Confucius Temple. In the main hall is a shrine to Confucius; the other buildings have served as, among other things, a state-administered acad-

emy that lasted through several dynasties. Originally built in 1034, the temple has been destroyed and then rebuilt time and again. Much of the stonework from the most recent rebuilding in 1986 is original to the Qing construction of 1869, which was burnt down by the Japanese.

有朋自远方来 不亦乐乎

仁者不忧 知者不惑 勇者不惧

The temple grounds were once massive, including what are now streets full of restaurants and tourist markets to the east and west. The entrance lies under a massive arch on a plaza giving onto the Qinhuai River in the southern part of Nanjing. Passing through the Gate of the Great Saint, one encounters a walkway lined with statues of Confucius' most famous disciples leading to what is said to be the largest statue of him in all of China, more than six meters tall.

不学礼 无以立

己欲立而立人 己欲达而达人

Behind the shrine is a large room decorated with a series of scenes from Confucius' life done in low relief with marble and semiprecious stones. These scenes purport mainly to show Confucius embodying the virtues of etiquette, decorum and wisdom.

己所不欲 勿施于人

In a second courtyard behind the main hall there are small pavilions to either side, one holding a large bell and the other a drum. Around the inner edge of this courtyard is a series of rooms, most of which are filled by an exhibition naturally entitled "Chinese Culture and Courtesy Throughout History."

Artifacts

The Jiangsu Provincial Museum is rich in artifacts from the two phases of the Song dynasty. It has a gold-plated silver statue of a reclining Buddha, a coffin made of solid gold, and an outer coffin made of silver, all from the Northern Song. There are several beautiful embroideries from the Southern Song, including an extraordinary piece showing the fifth-century Indian monk Bodhidharma harnessing magical powers in order to float across a river, and another, more delicate piece showing three quail near a grove of bamboo. There are calligraphic scrolls including a letter by Zhu Xi in cursive hand, and paintings on spun silk, most notably the "Ox-grace in Four Seasons" by Yan Ciping. In jade, there is a beautiful green nephrite hairpin in the form of a crown with two tiny phoenixes carved at the bottom.

THE YUAN AND THE MING

元明1206–1644 A.D.

Key Historical Figures: **Hongwu** (洪武)
Jianwen (建文)
Yongle (永乐)
Zheng He (郑和)
Xu Da (徐达)

Historical Sites: **Xiaoling Tomb Complex** (孝陵墓)
Dongling Tomb (东陵墓)
Tombs of the Meritorious Ministers (明朝功臣墓)
Yangshan Stele (阳山碑材)
Tiansheng Natural Bridge (天桥)
Ming Palace Ruins (明故宫遗址)
Drum Tower (鼓楼)
Bell Tower (钟楼)
Xuanwu Lake (玄武湖)
Admiral Zheng He (郑和)
- **Heavenly Maiden Temple** (天妃宫)
- **Treasure-Ship Shipyard** (郑和宝船厂遣址)
- **Tomb of Zheng He** (郑和墓)

Bao'en Pagoda (报恩寺)
Zhonghua Gate (中华门)
Chaotian Palace (朝天宫)
Li Xiangjun Residence (李香君故居)

Map of Yuan and Ming Historical Sites (元明历史景点图)

After the Southern Song moved their capital to Hangzhou, Nanjing's political and economic status gradually declined. The arrival of the Yuan dynasty did little to change that, but in the middle of the fourteenth century, a young cowherd named Zhu Yuanzhang raised an army that by the year 1368 had vanquished the Yuan, sending the Mongols back to their homes on the steppes. Zhu changed his name to Hongwu, and took the throne as the first emperor of a new dynasty known as the Ming.

明城牆風光帶

Map of Ming-Dynasty Nanjing

Though Nanjing served as the Ming capital for only fifty-two years before the third emperor, Yongle, moved it to Beijing, those years brought extraordinary prosperity and growth to the region. However, in order for the city to be presentable as the capital of a new empire, it had to undergo a number of physical, political and administrative changes.

First, the city's name was changed yet again, this time to Yingtianfu (Answering Heaven). A new Palace City was built east of the old one, and the Temples of Heaven and Earth were raised south of Guanghuamen. A bridge was built over the moat to Hongwumen, the main entrance to the Palace City; running north from Hongwumen was a wide boulevard that ended at the entrance to the Forbidden City, which was laid out along lines later used for Beijing's own Imperial Palace.

The Ministry of Justice, the Censorate and the execution grounds were all built to the north of Xuanwu Lake. As has been noted, the city wall was greatly expanded, as was the Zhonghuamen fortress. In 1381, Hongwu began work on his own tomb on Purple Mountain—the only Ming tomb not located in Beijing. He died in 1398, and because the Crown Prince had preceded him in death, Hongwu was succeeded on the throne by his "Crown Grandson," Jianwen.

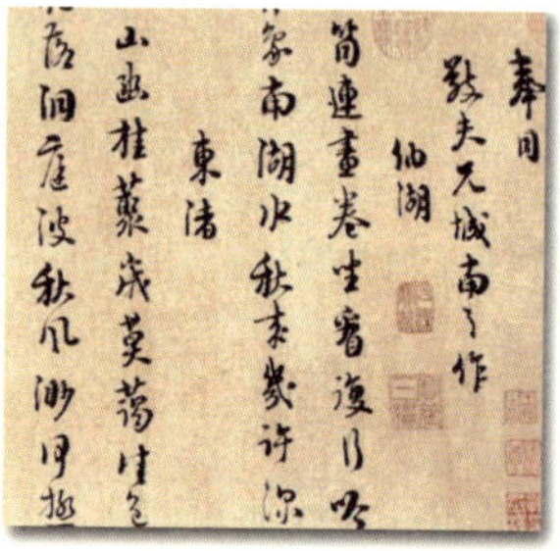

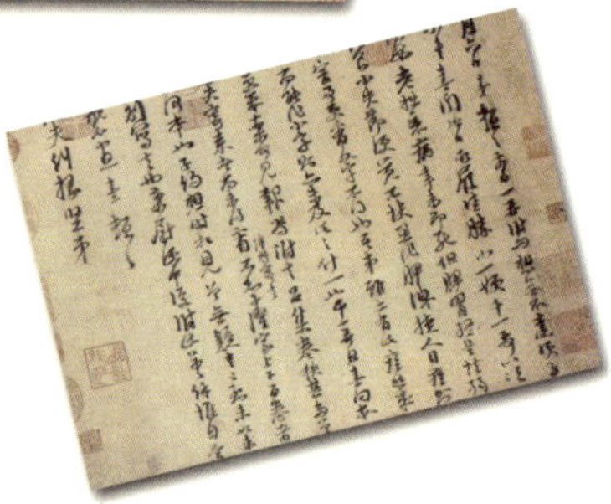

Jianwen was twenty years old at the time, and only lasted four brief and nervous years in power. By 1402, the Prince of Beijing—fourth son of the first Ming emperor, uncle of the second—had mustered sufficient military and political strength to make a bid for the throne. He marched on Nanjing, destroying much of it as he pushed through to the Forbidden City, and took power as Yongle, the third Ming emperor.

Yongle spent most of his life searching for Jianwen, who appears to have escaped as the city went up in flames, but never found him. And though Yongle did begin rebuilding the city he had destroyed, the work went unfinished, as he shifted the capital to Beijing nineteen years later. It was then that Nanjing first acquired its present name; it maintained a certain political and cultural importance throughout the rest of the Ming dynasty, but would not return to its position as the capital of a unified China for another four hundred ninety years.

Xiaoling Tomb Complex
(孝陵墓)

There are a large number of Ming sites worth visiting in Nanjing. Foremost among them is the Xiaoling Tomb complex, where the first Ming emperor is believed to be buried.

The tomb complex was built mainly by thousands upon thousands of criminals sprung from jail that their arms and backs might be put to better use, and is located at the southern foot of Purple Mountain. It is divided into four parts, each of which is separated from the others by stone bridges, in the interest of aesthetic beauty, divine favor and flood control. It begins at the Dismounting Archway to the far south, comes north to the Grand Golden Gate and Square Citadel, then becomes the Sacred Avenue proper, turning west-northwest along Stone Elephant Road, north again on Stone Warrior Road and then northeast past Plum Blossom Hill. Finally it reaches the entrance to the Tomb Palace, following directly north from there to the burial mound itself.

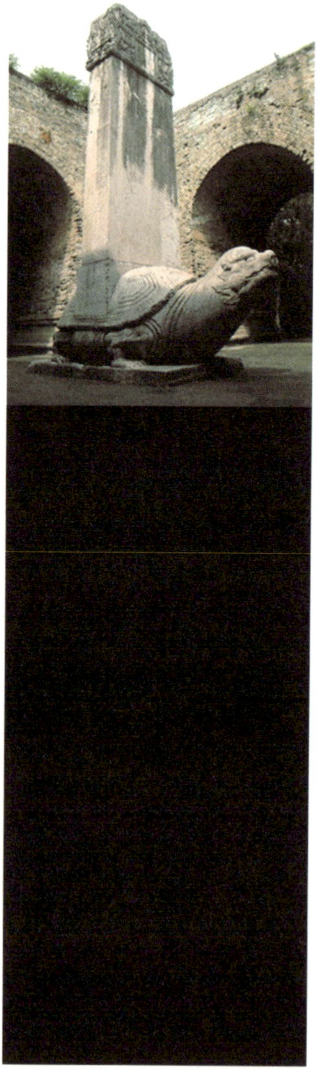

The Square Citadel holds the Tablet of Great Merits that Yongle erected in honor of the first Ming emperor in 1413. This tablet is immense, more than eight meters tall; nine carved dragons adorn its cap, and its eulogistic inscription, beautifully engraved in regular script, runs to 2746 characters. Like many memorial tablets, this one rests on the back of an improbably large tortoise, a mythological figure called Bi Xi, ninth son of the Dragon God.

The 1100-meter Sacred Avenue that begins here zigs left and zags right in response to topographical, historical and geomantic concerns. There is a small bridge over the first imperial river, and then two rows of massive stone animal sculptures serving as the vanguard of the tomb's protectors: six types of animal, two pairs of each. There are lions to represent power, xiezhi (a mythical creature with a mane and a unicorn's horn, its body built like a rottweiler the size of a rhinoceros) to represent justice, camels for wealth, elephants for strength, qilin (another mythical horned animal, this one with the scaly body of a dragon, a lion's tail, and ox's hooves) to represent peace and good fortune, and horses to represent servitude.

The avenue then turns north. Two hundred meters along is a high red wall in which is set the Tomb Palace gate, which was destroyed during the battle for Nanjing between the Taiping and the Qing in the 1860s, partially rebuilt a decade later, and wholly reconstructed in 1997. Inside, the path passes between the remains of the Imperial Kitchen and the Eastern Well Pavilion on the right, and the Wardrobe Hall and Western Well Pavilion on the left. Also of interest here is the Quechi, the Sparrow Pool, which used to be filled with food and water for the wild birds which, according to the booklet edited by the Xiaoling Tomb Museum, were necessary to protect the tomb "from the disturbance of ghouls and discarnate spirits."

Next comes the gate into the Imperial Tablet Hall, which holds five tablets erected by the Qing in honor of the first Ming Emperor—a gesture by the Manchu government to gain the support of the local Han population. The main tablet compares the Ming dynasty to the glory days of the Tang and Song. Off to one side of the gate is a small Qing reconstruction of the Sacrificial Palace first built by Hongwu. Of the original, only a section of the massive Sumeru pedestal (that name taken from what is, according to Buddhist literature, the tallest mountain in the world, home of Buddha himself) remains.

Passing first through the ruins of the Eastern and Western Side Halls (only plinth stones, corner post stones, doorways and stone aprons remain), and then among those of the fire altars used to burn paper money and the prayers read during sacrificial rites, one reaches the Inner Red Gate: the final separation between the world of the living and that of the dead. It could not be entered except by emperors, ministers with special permission, and eunuch guards in charge of incense, sacrifice and gardening.

Crossing the single-span Ascension Bridge, which is nearly sixty meters long and more than twenty-five meters wide, one reaches the immense front wall of the Rectangular Citadel. There is beautiful brick carving work on the splay walls west and east, and in places the lime used in the mortar has drained down to form small stalactites on the plinths. The architecture of this citadel is unique in Chinese history. The front wall measures sixteen meters high by seventy-five meters wide; it is also thirty-one meters thick, a fact that can only be appreciated by walking up through the tight dark tunnel that pierces it.

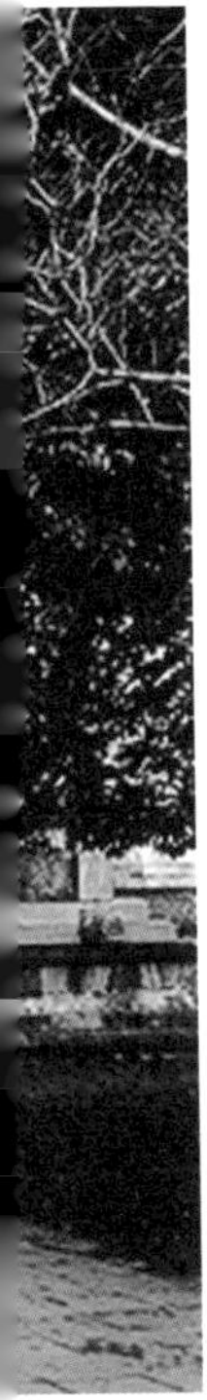

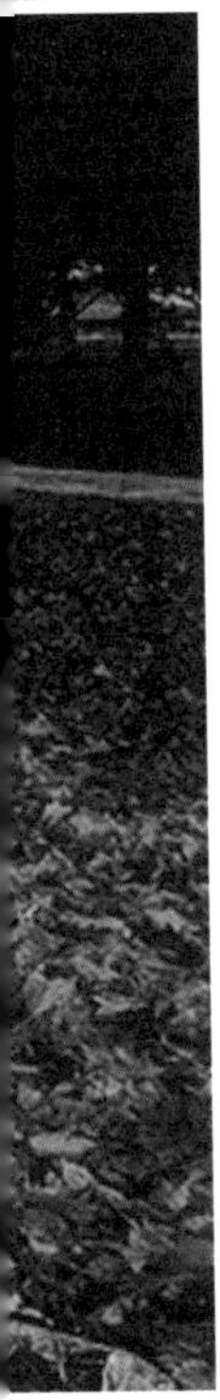

From the north side of the citadel sprouts a tremendous circular rampart wall seven meters high and more than a kilometer in circumference, with a single trail leading around its inner edge. Within that wall is a sharp manmade hill, now thickly covered in trees and undergrowth, called the Treasure Mound. It is nearly four hundred meters in diameter, and the first Emperor and his Empress are believed to be buried somewhere in an underground palace at its heart. A magnetic mapping of the mound has shown that there is indeed something underground, something very big, nearly 4500 square meters in area. But no one will know exactly what is there until the digging begins, if ever it does.

Dongling Tomb (东陵墓)

There are several other Ming sites worth visiting elsewhere on Purple Mountain. Sixty meters east of the Xiaoling tomb palace is the Dongling Tomb, built for Hongwu's eldest son, Crown Prince Zhu Biao. The tomb mimics the layout of Xiaoling, but is considerably smaller in scale. However, because Zhu Biao died at the age of twenty-five and never assumed the Ming throne, because his own son, Jianwen, only ruled for four years, and because the third emperor, Yongle, did everything in his power to erase Zhu's entire line (as well as those of his other brothers) from the imperial scrolls, the Dongling Tomb fell into politically-motivated oblivion, and stayed there until recalled to history by Qing emperor Qianlong in the middle of the eighteenth century.

Tombs of the Meritorious Ministers (明朝功臣墓)

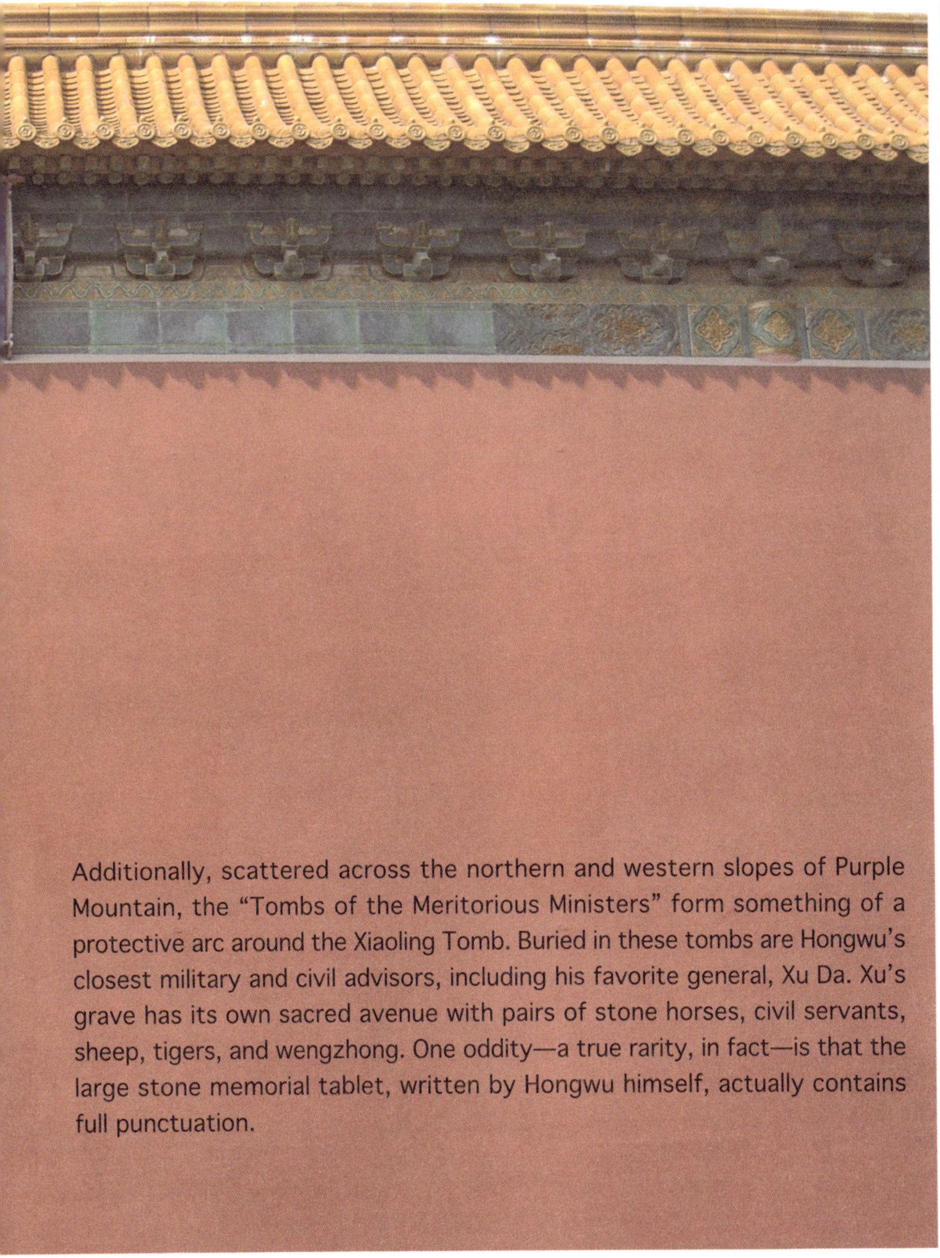

Additionally, scattered across the northern and western slopes of Purple Mountain, the "Tombs of the Meritorious Ministers" form something of a protective arc around the Xiaoling Tomb. Buried in these tombs are Hongwu's closest military and civil advisors, including his favorite general, Xu Da. Xu's grave has its own sacred avenue with pairs of stone horses, civil servants, sheep, tigers, and wengzhong. One oddity—a true rarity, in fact—is that the large stone memorial tablet, written by Hongwu himself, actually contains full punctuation.

Yangshan Stele (阳山碑材)

Purple Mountain is not the only location outside Nanjing where the remains of the Ming can be seen, and the extraordinarily large Tablet of Great Merits that Yongle erected in the Square Citadel is not even the largest such tablet he ordered carved. That honor goes instead to the Yangshan Stele, which to this day lies on its side on a hilltop twenty-five kilometers east of the city.

In August of 1405, a hundred thousand soldiers and carvers were brought to the Yangshan Quarry to begin work on the stele. Each mason was required to hand in thirty-three liters of stone cuttings every day; those who failed were executed and buried in the town below, whose name, Fentou, means "grave mound."

Simply put, the Yangshan Stele was designed to be far and away the biggest stone tablet in the history of the world. If fully assembled, it would reach a height of seventy-five meters, and would weigh twenty-six thousand tons. The foundation stone alone is seventeen meters high, thirty meters thick,

and twenty-three meters wide; the tablet stone clocks in at fifty-two meters high, four meters thick, thirteen meters wide; and the capstone is six and a half meters high, ten meters thick, and eighteen meters wide.

It was only after the workers cut the tablet stone and tried to maneuver it that they realized they were attempting the impossible. They then cut a slab off of the foundation stone to form the Tablet of Great Merits. The Yangshan Stele would have been seven times larger.

Tiansheng Natural Bridge

(天生桥)

Out in Lishui County is another Ming site worth visiting: Tiansheng Qiao, a "natural" stone bridge created in 1368.

Among Hongwu's most pressing concerns upon taking the throne was that of rising water needs in and around his capital. He solved this problem by digging a canal connecting Shijiu Lake to the Qinhuai River, and thus to Nanjing. The canal is about eight kilometers long, and required the services of 80,000 men—soldiers, masons, prisoners—for almost ten years. This number of man-hours sounds preposterous given how short the canal is, until one sees the canal in person: in places it is thirty meters deep, and much of it is carved out of solid rock, including the Tiansheng Qiao section, where Hongwu decided to leave a single arc of stone in place above the watercourse.

The canal is still used by small barges transporting sand and stone for construction. Hongwu perhaps overstated the case when he declared it "as beautiful as a small Three Gorges," but the sheer rock faces in browns and grays, the bushes and vines trailing down the sides, the trees high on the upper banks and the stone bridge itself are all quite striking.

Ming Palace Ruins (明故宫遗址)

Within the city limits there are several more sites worth visiting, including what remains of the Ming Palace built by Hongwu at what is now Wuchaomen Park. The palace originally enclosed approximately five square kilometers, and was used for more than half a century by the first three Ming emperors. It had three large courtyards linking vast raised halls flanked east and west by altars and temples.

Burned to the ground by Yongle and only partially reconstructed, it was abandoned altogether when the Ming moved to Beijing; the Manchu looted it, and it was bombarded by Qing and Western troops during the Taiping rebellion. Now, apart from the Five Dragon Bridges there is nothing left but the enormous bases of the palace columns, and random fragments of the Meridian Gate. In 1997, all the loose stones were gathered, arranged in lines here in the park, and called the "Garden of Carved Stones from the Ruins of the Gate of Heavenly Worship."

Drum Tower

(鼓楼)

East of People's Square stands the Drum Tower, erected by Hongwu in 1382. The wooden superstructure was destroyed in the mid-seventeenth century; on a subsequent imperial tour, Qing emperor Kangxi paid a visit to the site and ordered both the reconstruction of the tower, later renamed The Monument Tower of the Qing, and the erection of the "Anti-Corruption Tablet" which now rests on the back of a tortoise at the heart of the tower, extending up through the ceiling of the first floor.

The first-floor architecture is beautiful, and there are two extraordinary wood sculptures glazed with bronze powder. Because these were carried out on the orders of Empress Dowager Cixi, the phoenix (symbolizing female imperial power) is carved on top, while its male counterpart, the dragon, is carved below—and the dragon is toothless. On the second floor, built around the tip of the tablet is a dining room stocked with original Qing mahogany furniture and furnishings; it is still a popular venue with Nanjing's governmental VIPs.

Bell Tower (钟楼)

Opposite the Drum Tower stands the Bell Tower, part of a pleasant hilltop complex; it's a small but handsome two-story pavilion, with a pointed roof and upturned eaves. Most of the buildings around it are restaurants and teahouses, and in the center there is a pond with a double-bridge in the form of a cross arcing over it.

The tower was originally located near Jingchuanmen, where it stayed well into the Qing dynasty. It had three bells, two of which were destroyed in the late nineteenth century; in 1889, the third one was emplaced here by Xu Zhenwei, governor of this region. The bell was cast in 1389 during the reign of Hongwu, is three and a half meters high and weighs 23,000 kilograms. It has an interesting purple-brown hue, and according to Nanjing locals, when it is rung, the sound produced seems to be a voice saying, "My shoes, my shoes!"

The story: the first several attempts to cast this bell failed, so Hongwu had the bellsmith executed. The daughter of the bellsmith was so distraught that she then took off her shoes, arranged them neatly on the platform, and jumped into the mold just as the bronze was being poured for one final, and ultimately successful, attempt.

玄武湖

Xuanwu Lake (玄武湖)

Xuanwu Lake, in northeastern Nanjing, is of interest for at least two reasons pertaining to the Ming. For one, on the south side of the lake is the Wumiao Sluice Gate, built on the orders of Hongwu; the original stone slots through which the gates were lowered can still be seen.

Of greater interest, however, are the five islands that rise from the waters of the lake. These islands had served for centuries as a place of retreat and refuge for imperial families, but under the Ming they became something far more important, albeit rather less sexy: the site of the imperial tax and census archives.

玄武湖

In 1381, Hongwu ordered that all tax records, household registrations and property census results be brought here; the majority of them were lodged in what is now the Archival Museum on the northernmost island. He believed that having the scrolls on an island would make it easier to control access to them, and to defend them from the twin dangers of fire and mice. The documents were kept here for more than three centuries.

In 1490, the archive held 772,900 volumes of records, but by the end of the Ming dynasty in 1644, only 170,000 volumes were left: a combination of rot and rodents had dispatched the rest. And as the books fell apart, the system did as well; too many people were now cheating with impunity. The entire archive was abandoned when the Qing took power.

Sidebar: Zheng He (郑和)

The first two Ming emperors, Hongwu and Jianwen, distrusted the eunuch caste and diminished its role in court affairs, trusting instead to the advice of their Confucian mandarins. However, the third emperor, Yongle, reversed that state of affairs, and turned to a eunuch—to a Muslim eunuch of Mongol blood, no less—to oversee several of the most important projects he undertook.

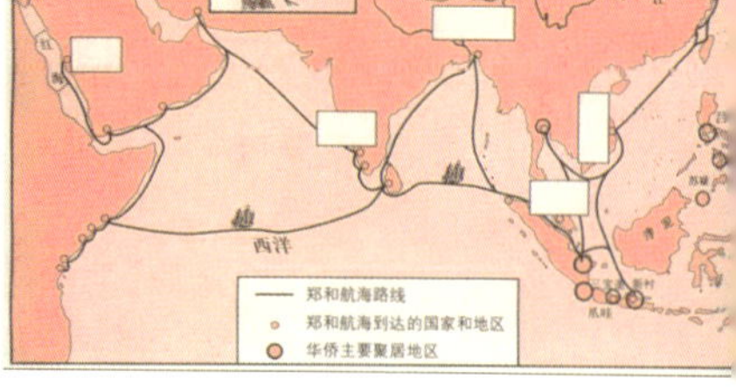

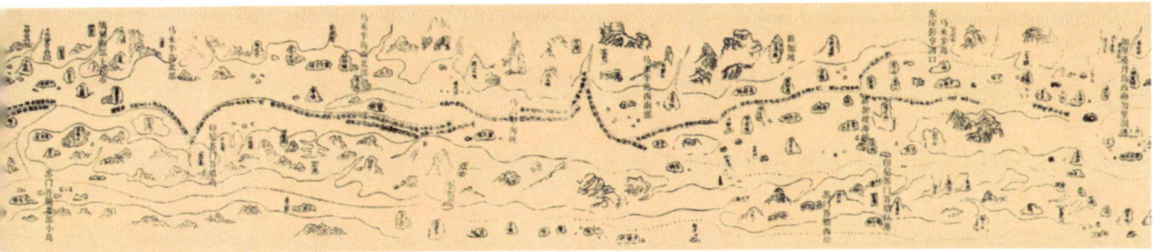

Over the course of the twenty-eight years from 1405 to 1433, that eunuch, now known as Admiral Zheng He, made seven voyages to more than thirty countries in Asia, Africa and the Middle East. British author Gavin Menzies has argued that he reached the Americas as well; that debate rages on, as does the debate over the authenticity of several maps involved in Menzies' thesis, but it now appears that if China had not turned inward halfway through Zheng He's sixth and penultimate voyage, he might indeed have charted the New World.

The numbers on the fleet Zheng He commanded are astounding by any measure, and put to shame the comparatively miniscule efforts taking place in Europe and elsewhere at the time: he had more than three hundred ships at his disposal, a crew totaling 28,000 men, and traveled more than 100,000 kilometers all told. The Treasure Ships were nearly one hundred forty meters long, and fifty-six meters wide at the beam, with nine masts, twelve sails, rudderposts that could be raised as needed in shallow waters, sixteen internal watertight compartments, and a cargo capacity of seven thousand tons. They were accompanied by agile warships, smaller patrol boats, massive horse transports, grain ships carrying 1,200,000 kilograms each, and water ships each bearing 1000 hogsheads, enough for 1000 people to survive a year without touching land.

From his first voyage in 1405 to his fifth in 1417, Zheng He's military, diplomatic and trading skills ensured that the Treasure Ships returned with an extraordinary variety of goods and living creatures, including "dragon saliva" (since identified as ambergris), amber, zebras and oryx from Africa; gold cloth and gems from India; parrots, sandalwood and cardamom from Thailand; and leopards, gold and silver from Korea. From Somalia to Indonesia, sites where he landed were renamed in his honor. Along the way, his fleet brought many foreign kingdoms into the Chinese tribute system, according to which they paid dearly in local luxuries in return for protection and trading privileges, including sharp discounts on highly valued Chinese goods such as silk, porcelain, medicine and lacquer ware.

Unfortunately, only two years into his sixth voyage, Zheng He and his fleets were called home. Yongle succumbed to illness in the course of a poorly planned and entirely unnecessary expedition against the Mongol emperor Arughtai, and in 1424 his son took the throne under the name Hongxi. Immediately upon assuming power, Hongxi ordered that the Treasure Ship voyages cease; that no more such ships be built, or even repaired; that foreign trade come to an end.

That sixth voyage was by most measures a success, but by the time the ships lowered anchor in 1423, the Chinese powers-that-be had lost interest in the outside world. The mandarins, seeing no real benefit in dealing with "barbaric" foreign nations, openly scorned the returning admirals, with the exception of Zheng He himself, but even he was relegated to the position of Nanjing harbor master. Hongxi died after only a year on the throne, but his son, who ruled as Xuande, only intensified Hongxi's policies. In the interest of social harmony, the merchant class was reined in, and the landed gentry regained the political and economic power they had previously enjoyed.

Xuande allowed Zheng He to make one last voyage in 1430, this one to Mecca, but the great navigator, now sixty-four years old, took sick on the return trip and died somewhere off the coast of India. It appears that his body was lowered into the water, and China's storied age of naval exploration came to a close.

Shortly thereafter, the records of those seven voyages disappeared as well: a mandarin named Liu Daxia who worked at the Ministry of War seized the archives, condemned them as pointless, and burned them. Over a period of time, the fleet was broken up and the overseas colonies were abandoned. Multi-mast, ocean-going ships were banned, as was learning a foreign language or teaching foreigners to speak Chinese. These policies were kept in place to the end of the Ming dynasty, expanded still further under the Qing, and would not be overturned until early in the twentieth century.

Heavenly Maiden Temple (天妃宫)

There are several sites in Nanjing that bear witness to Zheng He's life and exploits. They are not all of equal historical value, but taken together they demonstrate the tremendous importance that he bears for this area, and this era of history.

The Tianfei (Heavenly Maiden) Temple is located on the west slope of Lion Hill near the Yangtze. It was erected in 1416 following Zheng He's return from his fourth voyage; the Heavenly Maiden, also known as Ma Tzu, is a Daoist ocean deity. This temple contains the Tianfei Palace, which holds a fantastically gaudy statue of Tianfei herself, and the Bodhisattva Palace, which has a slightly more somber statue of Yan Guang, the Far-Sighted Buddha. There is also a small pavilion holding a tablet erected in Zheng He's honor, and a small sub-palace.

Treasure-Ship Shipyard
(郑和宝船厂遗址)

A much larger site is the Zheng He Treasure-Ship Shipyard, which encloses part of the Longjiang yards where Zheng He's fleet was built. In their prime, these shipyards were the biggest in the world, employing more than 30,000 workers, and were connected to the Yangtze by a series of canals. Nearly 2000 artifacts have been excavated from Shipyard 6, a few of which are now on display.

In a Ming-style courtyard recently built to the right of the entrance, there is a green porcelain statue of Zheng looking very resolute, a map of his travels, and a few old wooden beams. There is also a four-

pronged Ming anchor standing a meter and a half tall, and a stone called the Yangtze Three Gorges Oval Stone, which bears a natural mineral formation that looks very much like a fleet of galleons sailing through the islands in the Yangtze.

In the innermost room there is a gigantic tiller nearly twelve meters long. Its size is impressive and the dark brown teak is beautiful, but there is little additional information. The display cases around it hold stone cannon balls, a nine-meter length of palm rope, metal nails and staples, and an assortment of wood fragments.

There are a few new bronze sculptures of Ming carpenters at work. A small bridge leads over a canal past a series of bamboo-strap bags of river stones like those once used as ballast; on the far side of the bridge is a life-size model of one of Zheng He's ships.

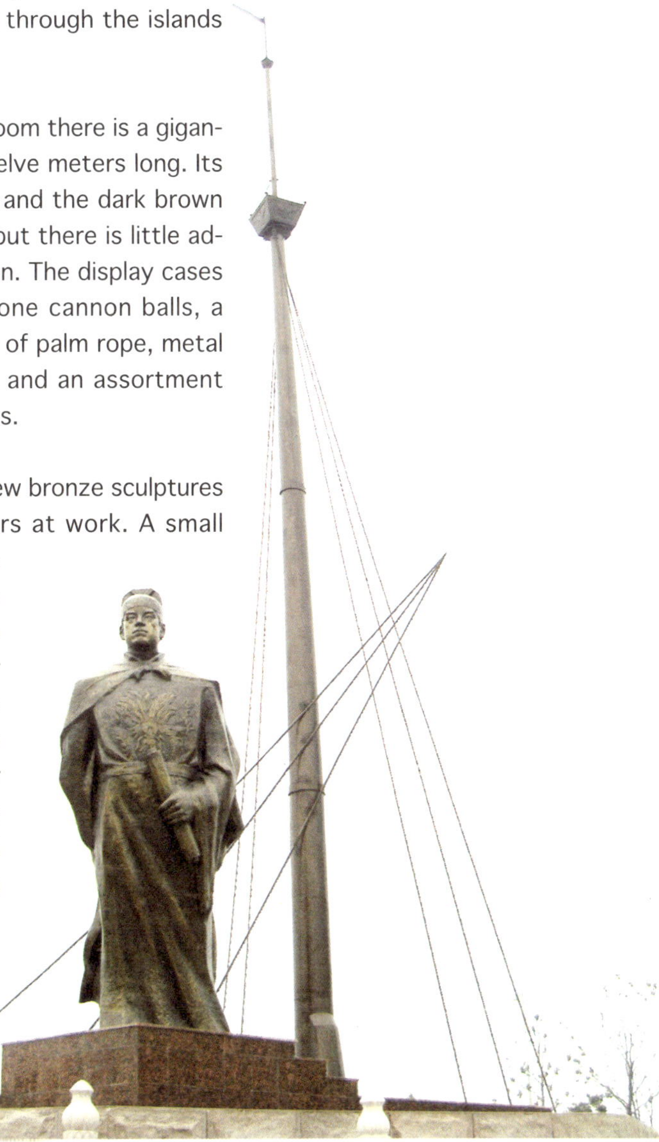

Tomb of Zheng He (郑和墓)

Finally, there is the tomb of Zheng He, which rests an hour south of the city in the Jiangning district, on the southern slope of Niushou Hill. It was reconstructed on the 580th anniversary of his first voyage, and is rarely visited; to the best of anyone's knowledge it contains only a set of his clothes, given his probable burial at sea.

The tomb is rather plain given the man's extraordinary achievements: a semi-circle of gray brick, a raised grass plot six meters wide and twelve long, and above that a stone coffin. The inscription at the foot of the coffin is in Arabic, and there is little other carving or design work of any kind.

Sidebar: Bao'en Pagoda

(大报恩寺塔)

One of the most extraordinary buildings ever constructed, the Bao'en Pagoda stood on a hilltop outside the southern gate of Nanjing for more than four hundred years before finally being destroyed during the infighting that took place toward the end of the brief reign of the Kingdom of Heavenly Peace. It was considered one of the Seven Wonders of the Medieval World, and was arguably the most significant architectural achievement of its time in China. Westerners who saw it compared it in grandeur to the Tower of Pisa, and even the Coliseum in Rome. Le Compte called it, "The best contrived and noblest structure of all the East."

Octagonal in shape, the pagoda rose nine stories into the air, to a height of seventy-eight meters. Begun by Yongle and finished in 1428 during the reign of his grandson, Xuande, it was visible for kilometers around, both during the day, when its glazed surface shone in multiple colors, and at night, when its hundreds of lamps were lit by the virgin boys who served as acolytes. It had four beautiful arched doors distributed from the second to the ninth floors, and hundreds of small niches filled with gold-plated statues of the Buddha.

It took sixteen years to build, cost 24.8 million silver dollars, and required the efforts of 100,000 craftsmen. The construction took so long in part because many new building methods first had to be invented; several of these methods have since been lost, and cannot be reproduced even with twenty-first century technology.

Inside the Bao'en Pagoda, and in the underground palace beneath it, many imperial treasures were stored: artifacts in gold and silver, silk brocade, and a copy of the Buddhist scriptures Xuan Zang brought back from India. Many scholars, including Director Zhou Daoxiang of the Imperial Examination Hall, believe that the scriptures and other treasures are still located in the palace: historical precedent holds that the value of the objects kept there should equal that of what is found above ground. The pagoda itself was of incalculable value; it was worth more, says Zhou, than the rest of Nanjing put together.

However, current plans do not include excavation of the underground palace. Instead, in cooperation with the Chen Guang Machinery Corporation, the city plans to level the entire area, including the several hundred houses in the vicinity, in part so that the pagoda can be rebuilt at a projected cost of more than 125 million dollars. Unfortunately, thus far the city has been unable to find a factory capable of reproducing the glazed bricks.

It is believed that in order to ensure that the pagoda would stand forever, the Ming ceramicists made three complete sets of the bricks, and put a series number on each brick to facilitate repairs. The first set was erected on site, and became the pagoda as it was known to history. The second set was placed in a storage facility nearby. The third set was buried secretly underground, as a complete replacement in case the tower was ever destroyed.

Though the tower was demolished by a renegade Taiping general, the second set of bricks was destroyed during the Great Leap Forward, and the third set has never been found, some bricks nonetheless survived: in 2004, in the course of building a new expressway to Shanghai, construction workers unearthed a number of them, which are now on display at the Imperial Examination Hall. Director Zhou believes they are from the ruins of the pagoda itself, given the centuries' worth of wear-and-tear in evidence. Also saved were the bricks from one of the pagoda's main doors. They were found in a minor temple near the city, and can now be seen in the Treasure Room at the Jiangsu Provincial Museum. Here the extraordinary colors and forms of the carved bricks have been brought back to life: the ivory-colored body of the elephant, the brilliant golden wings of the flying goat, the sharp black horns of the dragon, and the strange, almost alien countenance of the flying fairies.

Sidebar: Zhonghuamen (中华门)

The southern entrance to the city, known as Zhonghuamen, is by far the biggest of the thirteen gates built into the Ming city wall. The gate was begun by the Yuan in 1366, using the foundation of the original South Tang gate, but the Yuan did not get it finished in time to stop Hongwu's army from taking the city; it was then expanded, improved and completed by the Ming. The Qinhuai River serves as a moat both inside and out; to the south, the Rain Flower Terrace offers a certain amount of topographical protection.

Zhonghuamen is more properly considered a citadel than a gate: it has four separate gates of its own, and housed 3000 soldiers in the twenty-seven ambush niches scattered around the main structure. The outer wall is more than twenty meters tall and one hundred twenty meters in width. The citadel proper is one hundred twenty-eight meters deep, covering a total area of more than 15,000 square meters.

It is built of bricks, using mortar made of lime, tung oil and glutinous rice juice; as previously mentioned, each brick is stamped with its maker's name, so that any bricks that broke in the construction process could be promptly replaced by the responsible party. Each of the four inner gates is built into a separate arch, the largest of which is seven meters wide and almost sixty meters in length.

The slots in the roofs of these arches can still be seen; iron gates weighing 1000 kilograms each once slid down through them, trapping would-be invaders where, according to the citadel's brochure, they could be slaughtered "as easily as catching a turtle in a jar."

There are now rows of plaster soldiers in full battle regalia lining the two ramps that lead to the vast inner tower. A large wooden pavilion once stood at the top; it was burned down by the Japanese in 1937, but is presently under reconstruction.

Chaotian Palace (朝天宫)

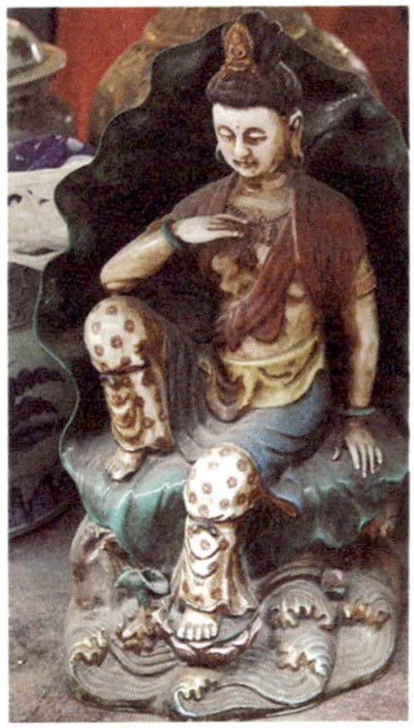

As has been noted, the Chaotian Palace belongs to many periods of Nanjing history, but it was under the Ming that it came to prominence, first as a center for ancestor worship, and later as a private temple and academy dedicated to Confucius. Still later it was used as a palace by the East King of the Taiping, Yang Xiuqing, and was burned to the ground when the Qing retook the city. The buildings as they stand were built near the end of the Qing dynasty.

In the main courtyard, there's a large statue of Confucius, and a heavy wooden gate. Flanking this courtyard on both sides is an antique market, the usual fascinating mixture of jade and marble and ceramic odds and ends. On the terrace above, a imperial throne has been set up such that tourists dressed as the emperor or empress might have their picture taken; the throne is also used as a set for many television programs. The main hall just beyond it, which currently houses the Nanjing City Museum, is said to be earthquake-proof: at the top of the pillars supporting the roof beams are dozens of outstretched "arms" called gongs cushioned with trapezoidal blocks called dou.

Li Xiangjun Residence
(李香君故居)

Early on in Kong Shangren's beautiful Kun opera *The Peach Blossom Fan*, a central character proclaims:

"The blossoms of the pear tree are fragile as snowflakes, the grasses faint as mist. Spring has conquered both banks of the river here where the courtesans dwell, each house graced by its own beauties.

I am Li Zhenli, the most splendid of the courtesans, whose renown surpasses that of all others. It was here that I was born, at this bridge of arriving and departure. Past glories have not faded here, nor has our opulence been tarnished."

The bridge of which she speaks, Wuding Bridge, is located in the heart of the Confucius Temple district, and the house owned and administered by the woman on whom her character was based has been nicely restored in recent years. It is a prominent two-story building with a fine balcony overlooking the Qinhuai; in its time it was known as Meixianglou, the House of Enchanting Fragrance, but it is now referred to as the Li Xiangjun Residence, named for Li Zhenli's most famous protégé.

Kong Shangren was a 64th-generation descendent of Confucius, but had gained little renown as a writer or scholar until *The Peach Blossom Fan* was published in 1699. The opera tells the story of Li Xiangjun's love for a handsome and brilliant young scholar named Hou Fangyu; it is set in Nanjing during the final stage of the collapse of the Ming empire, and the coterminous rise of the Qing. *The Peach Blossom Fan* brought lasting fame both to Kong and to Li Xiangjun, though by then she was dead and he would never again produce anything to match it.

Photo from Opera *The Peach Blossom Fan* (《桃花扇》剧照)

Li Xiangjun was first brought to Meixianglou as the three-year-old orphan of a Ming general, and her sympathies remained with the Ming empire even after it had disintegrated. She became famous in life for, among other things, her skills in the four classical arts (chess, calligraphy/painting, dancing/singing, and musicianship), her polished conversation, and her apparently otherworldly beauty.

The house's points of interest are as much architectural as they are historical. In the main upstairs hall,

the roof beams are beautifully carved, offering several illustrations of the elaborate word play involved at the intersection of Chinese architecture, social status, ritual, iconography and superstition. (To take but one example, the beam-carvings of elephants here are an acknowledgment and celebration of the house's social status, insofar as part of the word for elephant is 'xiang', which has a homonym meaning 'appearance', which is related to one's face, and social status is of course all about maintaining face.) There are also carvings of vases signifying long life, squirrels signifying abundant offspring, and fish for good luck.

Photo from Opera *The Peach Blossom Fan* (《桃花扇》剧照)

Li only lived here for twenty years or so, and there is some dispute as to how her life ended. Some say that she lived out her years as a Taoist nun in Qixia Temple, but according to Fu Banghua, the Nanjing scholar currently working as curator of the residence, Hou in fact carried Li away from the temple to his homeland in Henan. This has all the hallmarks of a happy ending, but Fu's research indicates that Li was rejected by Hou's illustrious family, and died of consumption or a broken heart—accounts vary—in an old and empty house. Another question concerns the gaps between the text of the play and its subtext, which involves Ming (and therefore Han) hatred of the Qing (Manchu) invaders. In later epochs, other nationalities have stood in for the Qing, as for example during the war against the Japanese that melded into World War II, when the story of Li Xiangjun was resurrected as a film, establishing her for all time as a patriot in the classic Chinese mode.

Artifacts

The artifacts remaining from the Ming dynasty are far too numerous for any but the most cursory list to be attempted here. In addition to the glazed door from the Bao'en Pagoda, the Jiangsu Provincial Museum holds some extraordinary work in porcelain, including a white meiping (literally "plum blossom vase," though this one was more likely used as a wine vessel) that was discovered under eleven meters of silt at the bottom of a well near an early Ming palace here in Nanjing. The inscription implies that it was a personal gift from Emperor Hongwu to a local official; it is the only such vessel ever found, and no one has any idea what it was doing at the bottom of a well.

Lacquer ware first became a national industry under the Ming, and there are a number of fine pieces here, including a set of carved Daoist emblems decorated with symbols formed of snakes. The back, top, and sides of the emblems all contain talismanic messages written in miniscule script likewise composed of snakes.

In gold, there are hairpins topped with beautiful filigree work in the form of peach blossoms and phoenixes, solid-gold earrings and spice-holders, and a hair-coil covering in filigree as thin as gauze.

In jade, there is a beautiful white cup with designs mimicking the zoomorphic ornaments commonly found on palace roofs, an intricate set of censor covers carved in openwork, and a lovely pair of interlinked rings from the fifteenth century. Finally, there is one of the most exquisite objects this author has ever seen: a most lifelike cicada of pure gold resting on a translucent jade leaf.

THE QING
清 1616–1911 A.D.

Map of Qing Sites (清代历史景点图)

Key Historical Figures:

Kangxi (康熙)
Qianlong (乾隆)
Hong Xiuquan (洪秀全)
Gan Xi (甘熙)

Historical Sites:

Taiping Rebellion Museum (太平天国)
Hong Xiuquan and the Kingdom of Heaven (洪秀全和太平天国)
Gan Xi Residence Museum (甘熙故居)
Jinhai Temple (静海寺)

The end of the Ming dynasty was brought about not by the succeeding empire, the Qing, but by a rebel warlord named Li Zicheng, in April of 1644. The final Ming emperor hung himself as Li's forces approached Beijing. An attempt to perpetuate Ming rule in Nanjing itself lasted less than a year, and the ranking Ming general, Wu Sangui, decided that he was better off fighting for the Manchu than against them. Too weak to confront the combined armies of Wu and the Qing, Li fled Beijing, and was dead at the hands of Manchu troops by the following summer.

The Manchu rulers then named Nanjing as the government seat for the viceroyalty of Liangjiang, which comprised what are now Jiangsu, Anhui and Jiangxi provinces. They also changed the city's name to Jiangning, meaning "The River Arrives Quietly."

One of the means by which the Qing hoped to maintain the peace that Nanjing's new name implied was by living separately from the Han Chinese they had conquered. Accordingly, they built new walls within many large cities to separate the Qing residential areas from the districts the Han were allowed to call home. In Nanjing, they walled in the old Ming palace city; according to the research of Kerk Philips, this wall ran north to south along what is now Longpan Road, and east to west along Houzaimen Street.

The governor then established his offices on the present-day site of the Presidential Palace.

Though modern sensibilities might find it odd, much of what is now urban Nanjing still consisted of open fields at that time, even within the outer walls, while large populated areas sprang up outside those walls. The northwestern part of the city was mainly gardens and barracks, while the area immediately south of Zhonghuamen was heavily populated and included many of the city's most important temples. The wealthiest citizens lived mainly on the banks of the Qinhuai and in what is now the greater Confucius Temple district.

The manner in which the country had turned inward, beginning with the fourth Ming emperor and continuing through nearly three centuries of Qing rule, did not stand the Chinese in good stead when the British came sailing up the Yangtze in the early 1840s, determined, among other things, to force the Chinese to continue the opium trade. The battles were rather one-sided, as were the agreements signed to end them: the Treaty of Nanjing was only the first of the "unequal treaties" which together obliged the Qing to open a number of Chinese ports, pay massive indemnities, and cede ownership of Hong Kong to Great Britain.

Taiping Rebellion Museum

(太平天国)

What was once an extensive garden built by Ming emperor Hongwu for General Xu Da later became the Zhanyuan Imperial Palace. According to Jonathan Spence, it was built in honor of Yang Xiuqing(杨秀清), the West King of the Taiping. However, it is generally believed that the palace was used instead by the East King, Yang Xiuqing, and it is certain that Yang himself never lived here; though he had been of tremendous importance as the vessel through which Jesus Christ spoke to the Heavenly Kingdom in the early years of the rebellion, he was killed during the ultimately unsuccessful siege of Changsha, six months before the Taiping arrived in Nanjing.

The palace was destroyed along with the rest of the city when the Qing retook Nanjing, but in 1958

it was rebuilt as the Taiping Rebellion Museum. The museum focuses both on the rebellion itself and on the attempts of the Heavenly Kingdom to rule the vast area of southern China over which it had control, however briefly.

Hong Xiuquan
洪秀全

Just inside the main hall is a ferocious bronze statue of Hong Xiuquan, the Heavenly King himself. Farther inside, there is a display of seals and coins issued by the Taiping, as well as maps showing their steady progress toward Nanjing from their original base in Guangdong Province. There are also texts describing Taiping attempts at legal, social and agrarian reform beginning with their arrival in Nanjing in 1853, and placards discussing the eventual splintering of the Taiping leadership, the siege of the city by Manchu and foreign forces, and the Qing re-conquest of the city in 1864.

Still farther into the hall is a set of displays holding some of the weapons used by the Taiping, including muskets, pistols, and some magnificent halberds. Other exhibits detail inventive battle tactics and formations designed by the Taiping, such as the Crab Formation, the Snake Formation, and the Hundred Bird Formation. Among other objects of interest, there is a Taiping bugle made of a seashell, and a lacy undershirt made of strips of bamboo.

In back of the main hall there is a small and pleasant labyrinth of terraces and walkways, rock gardens and ponds, and several small pavilions, including one which was heated from below to keep the Heavenly King warm while he played chess. On one outer wall there is a beautifully carved character for the word "tiger," from the hand of Weng Tonghe, a noted late-Qing calligrapher and would-be reformer. There is also an entire hall devoted to recent drawings and calligraphy and paintings celebrating the Taiping, all done by schoolchildren.

Sidebar: Hong Xiuquan and the Kingdom of Heavenly Peace

(洪秀全和太平天国)

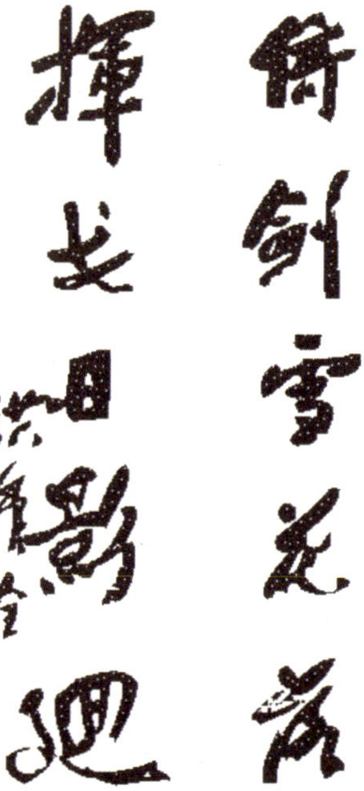

Destiny appeared to have prepared Hong Xiuquan for the life of a schoolteacher, or a scholar, or perhaps a minor official in the regional administration of Guangxi Province in southern China. Then something else came along. By the time his life ended at the age of fifty, he had gathered a tiny group of friends and family members and raised himself to a position of godhead in their eyes, had grown them into an army more than a million strong, and had at last established the capital of his Heavenly Kingdom here in Nanjing. However, in so doing he was responsible for the deaths of approximately twenty million Chinese.

In 1836, at the age of twenty-four, Hong traveled to Guangzhou to take the regional-level Imperial examination; he failed, but on the street outside the examination hall he was given a set of tracts written by a recent Christian convert named Liang Afa. Apparently without taking the tracts to heart, Hong returned to his studies, and took the exam a second time the following year. Again he failed, and this time he fell sick, arriving home feverish, nearly delirious. Once safely in his bed, he fell asleep, and had the dream that would transform Chinese history: he was taken up to Heaven, purified, and blessed by a woman he later identified as his Holy Mother; he was then given a sword and a gold seal by his Holy Father, who allowed him to do battle with the hundreds of demons who had tricked their way into Heaven, and then with the demons on earth.

Over the next seven years Hong failed the exam several more times. Only then, in the summer of 1843, did he turn to the tracts he'd been given in Guangzhou. As he read them, he remembered the dream that he'd had, and came to believe that he was, quite literally, the second Son of God. He began preaching his understanding of Christianity in and around his village, and quickly gained his first four converts; all of them lost their jobs the next year for preaching against Confucianism.

Hong and three of his disciples then traveled more than five hundred fifty kilometers to the area around the Guangxi town of Sigu. In a few months of preaching there, they brought in a hundred more converts, nearly all of them of the Hakka minority, like Hong himself.

Their increasing militarism, expansive growth and bizarre beliefs soon drew the unfavorable attention of the Qing government and army, and Hong began looking for a more easily defendable base. Over the next sev-

eral years the Taiping forces grew stronger and stronger as they made their way toward Nanjing, raiding undefended towns and destroying temples along the way. In mid-March, their numbers now having reached half a million troops, they broke in through the northwest side of the city wall, and scaled the southern side near Zhonghuamen. They poured into the city, destroying much of it as they did so; the following day they massacred the five thousand troops and thirty-five thousand civilians who had taken shelter in the Palace City's inner citadel.

Hong sought to turn feudal China into a modern (in some senses) country through land redistribution, a common granary, education and legal reform. Men and women were equal before the law: it was only under the Taiping that women were allowed to sit the imperial examinations now based primarily on the Bible rather than the Confucian classics, and women fought as brutally and died as bloodily in his armies as did any of the men. Foot-binding was banned, and a classless society was sought.

Unfortunately, none of these goals was attained for any length of time. In the end, the rules were applied savagely in the cities and rarely in the rural areas, with great attention paid to the armed forces and little to the sort of civil government that could have improved the lives of his subjects. Hong failed to ally with similar anti-Qing movements, and neglected to inform the foreigners in Shanghai that their recently won economic gains were in no danger from him; his assault on the city was turned back at great loss, and the Qing troops pursued him all the way back to Nanjing. Additionally, infighting among his own generals led to a bloodbath in which tens of thousands of people were slaughtered, and to the deaths of several of his finest advisors.

The siege of Nanjing conducted by the combined forces of the Qing and the foreign-led Ever-Victorious Army grew tighter and tighter, and Hong sequestered himself in his palace. By December of 1863, with the Taiping supply routes cut, their gates blockaded and their bases elsewhere destroyed, the situation in Nanjing was beyond desperate. When there was no food left anywhere in the city, Hong declared that weeds would turn to manna in the mouths of the faithful. Eating some himself, he promptly fell sick. By the first of June he was dead, and the Heavenly Kingdom followed him to the grave only a few months later.

Gan Xi Residence Museum

(甘熙故居)

Just south of Zhongshan Road lies the Gan Xi Residence Museum, a beautiful Qing-era family complex that is approximately two centuries old. The official name of this site is "Ganjia Dayuan and the Museum of Ancient Necessities." The Gan family itself referred to their house as "Ninety-Nine-and-a-Half-Rooms Hall," in response to the emperor's decree that no family residence could have more than one hundred rooms. In reality, the house contains well over three hundred rooms and interior courtyards, with a total area of nearly six thousand square meters.

Gan Xi (1797-1852), also known as Shi An, was a famous Qing scholar and bibliophile. He authored several texts still read today, including *Trifles in Baixia*, *Essays on Tong Yin*, and *The Historical Record of Qixia Temple*. The residence was first built by his father, but Gan Xi oversaw its considerable expansion. Recent restorative work is in most places very good, though many of the historical displays lack sufficient information.

Among the main rooms, Yougong Hall contains a beautiful mahogany altar with several small but colorful Qing-era ceramic statues of Daoist deities. Drama Lovers' Hall is where the family gathered to enjoy Kun and Peking opera; several members of the Gan family were quite famous as opera singers and actors, and the family was and continues to be very generous in its support of the arts. Finally, there is the Wedding Room, perhaps better translated as Honeymoon Suite, with its massive bed, beautiful red tapestries and paper cuttings on the walls.

The above description concerns only half of the house as it now stands. The other half is dedicated to a folk art museum and a music school.

Jinghai Temple
(静海寺)

It has long been the tradition of conquering nations to search out the sites of greatest symbolic importance to the peoples they have conquered, and then to use those sites in various ways to further deepen the humiliation felt by the defeated. To give only one example, invading forces throughout the world have seen fit to tear down old temples, and to rebuild new ones dedicated to other gods on the same site, in many cases using the same bricks.

Something along these lines occurred in August of 1842 at the Jinghai Temple, located next door to the aforementioned Tianfei Temple. The treaty ending the first Opium War was signed in the captain's quarters of the HSS Cornwallis, anchored on the Yangtze just west of the temple, but the negotiations leading up to it occurred here. The temple buildings then standing, themselves reconstructions of the originals that had been torched after Zheng He's death, were subsequently destroyed, partly by the Taiping and partly during the Cultural Revolution. The temple has since been restored yet again, and is now the Nanjing Treaty History Museum; prior to the return of Hong Kong to China, it was the site of several large and angry gatherings. It now has a small collection of photographs, maps and newspaper clippings related to the Opium Wars and the treaties that followed them.

One sign says, “The scene of negotiation is partly restored just to warn the people of the past.” While this is perhaps a bit ambiguous, the more ominous tone of another sign speaks more clearly to present-day China’s growing confidence in its own power: “We shouldn’t forget the national humiliation in the past century. In order to warn the world, we arranged the exhibition to encourage each other.”

Artifacts

The Gan Family Residence Museum has a very nice display of the family's dozens of red clay teapots from the Ming and Qing dynasties, and in their Heirloom Hall, there are a great many displays containing lockets and vases and ivory boxes, fans and hairpins, and embroidered objects of all kinds, ranging from bibs to fan cases to mirror sheaths. Perhaps the most beautiful piece is an ivory name-card holder, which bears an unbelievably intricate carving of an old house in a bamboo forest. There is also a fine stone carving of a bixie, and a bamboo pillow shaped like a tiny coffee table.

Meanwhile, the Jiangsu Provincial Museum holds a vast collection of Qing artifacts, including many from the dynasty's artistic peak in the eighteenth century. There is a large number of spectacular red lacquer ware vases and boxes, and a throne with beautiful inlay work in gold and black lacquer, originally used by the Qing emperor in his summer palace at Chengde, north of Beijing.

Finally, porcelain took on a much larger role in imperial and daily life under the Qing than it had in any previous dynasty; by the middle of the eighteenth century it had largely replaced the gold, silver, jade, wood, bamboo and lacquer ware pieces earlier employed. Among the pieces on display, there are a few from the Kangxi period (1665-1680), when the Imperial Kiln was still in the process of recovering from the chaos of the early Qing years; one of these is a softly elegant "peach bloom water pot" with incised dragons on all sides. However, Qing porcelain truly came into its own during the Qianlong era (1680-1795), and most of the pieces here come from that period. There is a slender hexagonal vase with beautiful dragon designs in underglaze blue on a bright yellow ground, produced for Emperor Qianlong's sixtieth birthday celebration. There is also an incredible blue and white zun vase covered with no fewer than 10,000 characters for the word "longevity," written in six major calligraphic styles.

THE REPUBLIC AND THE WARLORDS

中华民国和军阀割据时代

1911–1949 A.D.

Key Historical Figures: **Sun Yat-sen** (孙中山)

Chiang Kai-shek (蒋介石)

John Rabe (约翰·拉贝)

Historical Sites: **Sun Yat-sen Mausoleum** （中山陵）

Linggu Pagoda （灵谷塔）

Memorial Hall of the Nanjing Massacre
（侵华日军南京大屠杀遇难同胞纪念馆）

Plum Village （梅园新村）

Rain Flower Terrace Martyrs Museum （雨花台烈士纪念馆）

Presidential Palace （总统府）

John Rabe Residence （约翰·拉贝故居）

Republican-era Architecture （民国建筑）

Map of Republican Historical Sites
(中华民国军阀割据时代历史景点图)

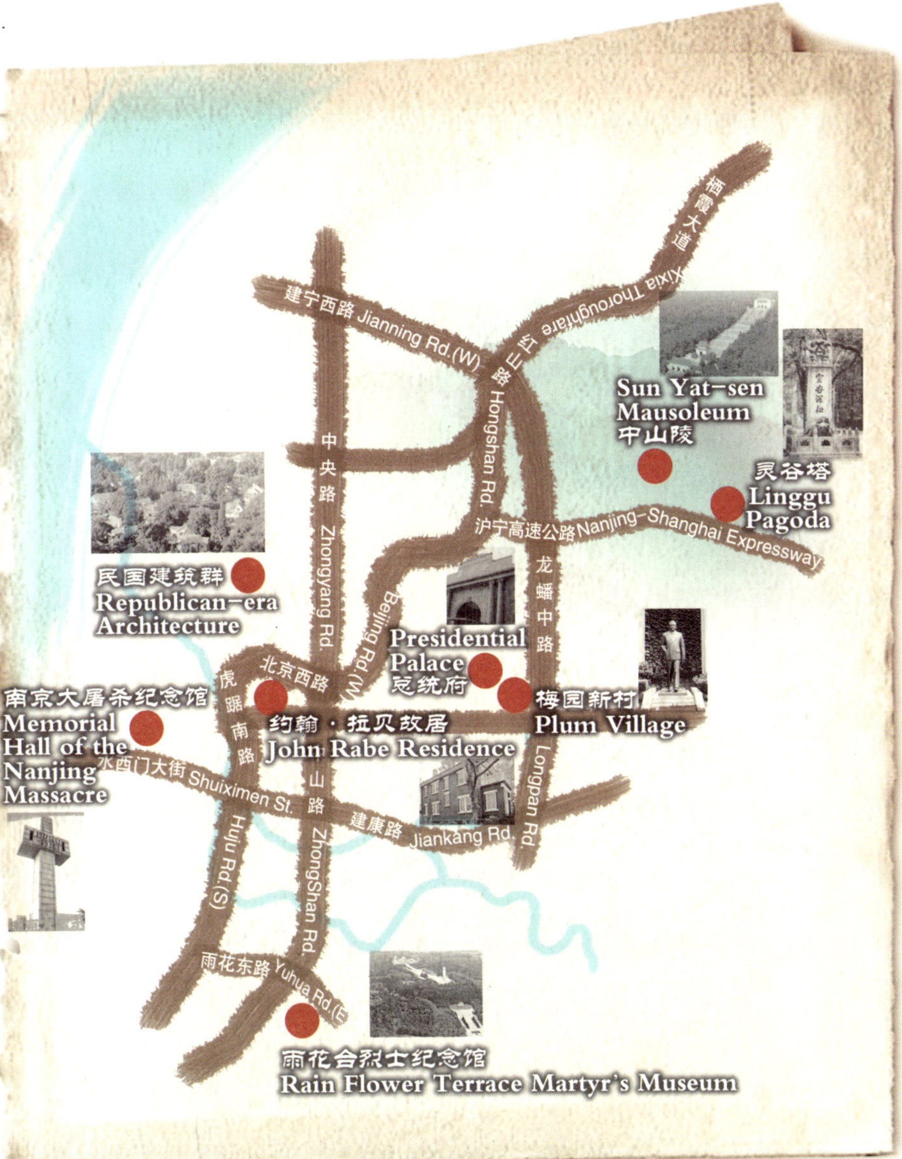

The fatal weaknesses of the Qing dynasty, amply demonstrated at the Treaty of Nanjing and by the Taiping insurrection, resulted in the total collapse of Manchu rule in 1911; Nanjing was taken by Nationalist troops in December of that year after weeks of heavy combat. 1911 was also the year that the old Ming name for the city was resurrected once and for all. As the population grew wealthier, Nanjing's economy gradually shifted from one focused on production to one spurred by consumption. By the early 1930s, the food, service and entertainment industries were out-earning those of manufacturing and agriculture.

The Republican period began with Dr. Sun Yat-sen, one of the leaders of the revolution, elected as Provisional President; he established the Guomindang government back in Nanjing, raising his offices on the grounds of the former Taiping Palace. Following the abdication of the last Qing emperor only three months later, Sun withdrew from office and the next president, a warlord named Yuan Shikai, whose instincts were less than democratic, moved the capital once more to Beijing in 1912. The following year, Nanjing was briefly occupied by a general named Zhang Xun. This was the beginning of the bafflingly complex era known as the Warlord period, with various armed groups fighting one another for the right to lead China, and with Sun briefly assuming the presidency in altered form twice more over the following twelve years.

After Sun's death in 1925, Chiang Kai-shek had complete control over the Nationalist movement. The Guomindang government had some success in rebuilding China's administrative, educational and transportation infrastructure, but those achievements were primarily urban in nature. The rural areas stayed as poor as they had ever been, a situation that Mao Zedong used to his advantage as he built up strength in northwestern China following the Long March from his earlier bases in Jiangxi.

As Chiang grew more and more obsessed with obliterating Mao's army, the Japanese continued their steady encroachment on Chinese territory. Throughout the early 1930s, there were massive protests in Nanjing and elsewhere against Tokyo's repeated demands for still more land. Then in December of 1936, Chiang was captured by his own generals while in Xi'an; he promised them that he would form a unified government with the Communists and other groups, but before that could happen, the Japanese invasion came in full force.

The Guomindang government fled first to Wuhan, and later to Chongqing. The Nationalist army followed not far behind, and in what is still known as the Rape of Nanking, in six weeks the Japanese slaughtered about 300, 000 Chinese. (The exact figure is a matter of some debate. In the early 1930s, the city's population was only about 250,000; however, by 1937 Nanjing and its suburbs held nearly a million people, most of them refugees fleeing the Japanese advance.) They also raped thousands of women of all ages, and burned down a great deal of the city long after it had surrendered.

When World War II was over, Nanjing was again the nation's capital from 1945 to 1949; after a brief attempt at reconciliation, the Communist forces and the Nationalist army spent the rest of those four years at war. The Guomindang government was further weakened by inflation and infighting; unemployment in Nanjing reached thirty percent in 1946.

By September of 1948, some 20,000 students were reduced to begging in the streets of Nanjing, and soon turned their anger on the sitting government. Chiang resigned in January of 1949 and fled to Taiwan, leaving the country in the hands of Li Zongren. Three months later the city surrendered to the approaching Communist forces. Mao declared the establishment of the People's Republic of China on October 1st, by which point the capital had already moved back to Beijing, where it has remained ever since.

Sun Yat-sen Mausoleum
(中山陵)

While the Xiaoling Tomb complex dominates the south-central slope of Purple Mountain, it is the tomb of Sun Yat-sen which dominates the southeastern side: his Mausoleum Scenic Park, started in 1926 and finished in 1931, covers a total of almost one hundred forty hectares. Sun is universally recognized as the father of modern China. His tomb is visited by great numbers of pilgrims from elsewhere on the mainland, and has equal significance for visitors from Taiwan: it is a shrine to their sovereign, a reminder of how things might have been had he lived long enough to assume power once more before his death of liver cancer in 1925.

孙中山

Sun Yat-sen

Seen from the air, the mausoleum area has the shape of a bell. According to a sign near the top, the bell tolls to this day as a warning: the sign speaks of Sun's "devotion (...) to the cause of waking up the masses and saving the Chinese nation and state." The design is credited to Lu Yanzhi, perhaps the most important of China's "first generation" architects, who studied at Cornell University and was mentored by Henry Murphy, an American architect responsible for, among other things, the Capital Plan which redrew the traffic arteries and distribution of Nanjing in 1929.

Nearby is the beginning of a Republican-style Sacred Avenue, which starts at the Memorial Archway of Universal Fraternity, built of white Fujian marble topped with blue-glazed tiles: the combination of blue and white throughout the mausoleum makes reference to the white sun and blue background of the Guomindang flag. From the archway, a stone staircase seventy meters wide and four hundred meters long leads up the forested slope to the main mausoleum gate, again built of white stone topped with blue tile.

Beyond the gate is a pavilion housing a stone stele six meters high: Sun's memorial tablet. From there it is steeper steps up another three hundred meters to the Memorial Hall. In the center of the hall is a statue of Sun carved in white marble by a French-Polish sculptor named Paul Landowski in 1930; the black walls around it are engraved in gold with a text Sun wrote called "Fundamentals of National Reconstruction." There is also a pillar holding his central slogan—"Everything for the People"—and the ceiling tiles form the flag of the republic that he helped to found (though he very nearly missed his own revolution: he was in the United States gathering funds when the ultimately successful 1911 revolt began in Wuchang).

Up slightly higher is the round Coffin Chamber. There is a marble sarcophagus bearing a sculpture of Sun lying in state, including wreaths of flowers carved at his feet. The coffin itself is located five meters below.

博愛

Linggu Pagoda

(灵谷塔)

Also found on Purple Mountain is the Linggu Temple Area, located slightly east of the Sun Mausoleum. Up past the massive steles on the backs of mythical turtles is another Memorial Archway, this one protected by two splendid white marble tigers, lithe and fast but frozen. As mentioned previously, many of the buildings here were built or have been coopted in the name of 20th century history. Beyond Beamless Hall is the nine-story Linggu Pagoda, built in 1934 on orders of Chiang Kai-shek. Designed by Henry Murphy, it is a memorial to Guomindang members killed during the battles of 1926-1928. It is impressive from a distance because of its height—nearly 60 meters—but only the progressively better views down the mountain make a climb up the stairs worthwhile. On the inside walls, the text of two speeches Sun gave at the Whampoa Military Academy were inscribed by four prominent Republican calligraphers.

南京大屠杀

Memorial Hall of the Nanjing Massacre

(侵华日军南京大屠杀遇难同胞纪念馆)

The Memorial Hall of the Nanjing Massacre is many things. It is, as its name implies, a memorial; it is also a museum dedicated to the darkest elements of human nature, and a killing field preserved behind glass. It is a necessary but not an easy place to visit.

The front courtyard holds a cross, a Peace Bell, and a number of bronze statues. As seen from here, it is clear that the angles of the memorial's walls and varied rooflines are all intentionally off square, producing a sense of imbalance in the viewer, almost of vertigo, the very surface of the earth gone unpredictable and strange.

The walkway leads to the left and up onto the Copper-plate Passage of Footprints, a path forty meters long holding the footprints of 222 victims of the Rape, and full-body sculptures of several more. Two of the sculptures are of women, one of whom was nine when she was bayoneted by the Japanese; she has the shoulder of her jacket pulled down to show the scar.

From there the walkway follows up and over into Graveyard Square, a huge courtyard divided into several sections. On this site, approximately 10,000 civilians and disarmed Chinese soldiers were executed. It is now mostly desolate bare ground with trees deliberately left to wither.

There are white cobblestones standing in for the bones of the dead, and a fringe of grass and living trees that a sign says represent resistance and vitality. And there is a statue called "Mother", based on a photograph taken by an American missionary named John Martin who was present in Nanjing before, during and after the Rape.

Around the edge of the courtyard are seventeen large raised stones, one for each of the city's main execution sites. Having circled it, one walks down a small hallway strung with pieces of origami: they are mainly strings of paper cranes nes tled into one another, left here by Japanese tourists. From here on in, all of the texts are in English, Chinese and Japanese, so that as many people as possible might be made to understand.

First one enters the Skeleton Display Room, a large plot of dirt enclosed with glass. The dirt is full of bones. There is little artifice in it: this was a pond where bodies were thrown, and they were discovered when the pond became a construction site decades later; the skeletons were exposed and the dig preserved. There were seven layers of bodies in the pond. Thirty-five of the skeletons are those of children. There are colored markers pointing things out: bones with bayonet marks and bullet holes, small skulls pierced with metal nails.

The museum proper has been built in the form of a bunker that rests beneath the hill one climbed for a first view of Graveyard Square. Its collection consists mainly of photographs. The carnage they show is unspeakably awful: civilians doused in kerosene or paraffin and torched; a head mounted on a fencepost; a child with his legs cut off; women raped and then disemboweled, their intestines stretched and bulbous and rotting in the sunlight.

And of course the great sickening irony: the vast majority of these photographs were taken not by Chinese victims or foreign witnesses, but by the Japanese themselves, who wanted souvenirs of their savagery, who were so foolish as to have the film developed at shops here in China, and in those shops were a few very brave people who risked their lives to make extra sets of the pictures. It is because of their bravery that past and present Japanese denials of the scale of the massacre here ring so very hollow.

And for all this, and for the hundreds of thousands of unphotographed deaths, and for the biological weapons trials conducted on Chinese captives here, a total of twenty-eight Japanese soldiers were convicted of war crimes. There are displays of this too: the three soldiers involved in a beheading competition, convicted by a Chinese war tribunal and executed on the Rain Flower Terrace in February of 1946; the two commanding officers, Matsui and Takeu, hanged in Tokyo in December of 1948. Finally, there is a statue of John

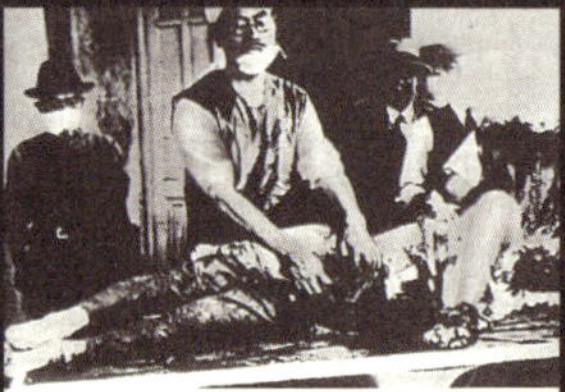

Above: Vivisection being performed on a Chinese victim by a Japanese biological warfare doctor.

上圖：日本細菌部隊的醫生正在進行的一場活體解剖。

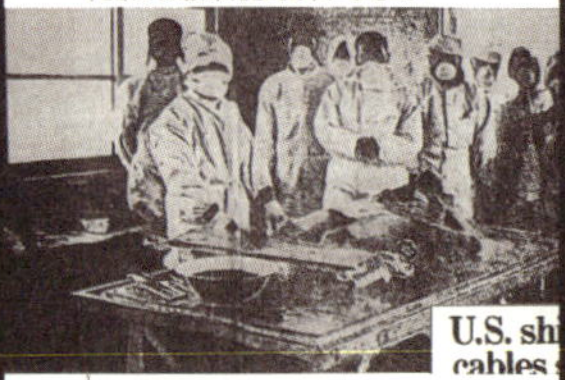

Above: A Chinese woman, raped and impregnated by a Unit 731 researcher, Kobayashi, is vivisected along with her fetus in the laboratory at Pingfang.

上圖：一個由七三一部隊的成員小林技手強姦而懷孕的中國婦女，連她腹中的胎兒一起被活活解剖。

Below: 1933. Severed heads of Chinese civilians in Lingyuan, in what is now Liaoning Province.

下圖：一九三三年在現遼寧西部的熱河凌源被日軍殘殺的中國人的頭顱。

Right: Severed heads of Chinese victims were displayed to intimidate onlookers and passersby in Tieling, Manchuria.

右圖：在遼寧鐵嶺被日軍砍下的中國人的頭顱被懸掛起來，恐嚇路人。

Courtesy of Shanghai Wenhua Publishing

Rabe—a small tribute to the bravery and higher instincts of this Nazi official known as the Oskar Schindler of China (see below)—and another devoted to Sino-Japanese reconciliation.

Left: Children of Longweishan, Manchuria, were bayoneted by Japanese soldiers. This picture shows their bodies about to be incinerated on piles of firewood.

左圖：[illegible]

Right: The Japanese High Command's 'positive' Chinese policy, inaugurated at Nanking, was carried out automatically by its troops throughout the war. This is spring 1938, a killing of a Chinese POW near Xuzhou, Jiangsu Province. Below: The same scene as in the photo on the right. The victim was already dead from repeated bayonet thrusts, but the target practice continued.

右圖：[illegible]

Left: Remains of victims of another massacre site in Chengde, Hebei Province.

左圖：[illegible]

Above: A village's ordeal: Civilians are buried alive by the invading Japanese troops.

上圖：[illegible]

Right: In preparing for the continuing war, even monks from Buddhist temples were subjected to military drill.

右圖：[illegible]

Above: A rank of tall, big-bellied sumo wrestlers, the popular traditional athletes, stands at dress right during a military drill in 1942.

上圖：[illegible]

Below: The domestic propaganda machine ground incessantly. Here the sounds of triumphal marching feet are relayed to radio listeners.

下圖：[illegible]

Left: A soldier ram[s a] bamboo spear in[to a] straw figure of Sir Winston Churchill[. A] placard on the s[...] urges passersby to stop and take a [...]

右圖：[illegible]

Right: Watched by uniformed middle-school students, drafted college students march in review in a rally at Meiji Stadium in Tokyo in October 1943. Some 650 of the college recruits would die as Kamikaze pilots.

右圖：[illegible]

Right: In the fever of militarism and "loyalty to the Emperor," when the China war drained Japan's manpower reserves, child "soldiers" drilled in Tokyo.

右圖：[illegible]

Plum Village

(梅园新村)

Meiyuan Xincun, slightly better known as Plum Village, was the site of the 1946-1947 attempt at peace talks between the envoys of the Guomindang and the Communist party delegation led by Zhou Enlai. Topics of discussion included future consultations between the two groups, an armistice agreement, and questions of troop reorganization. The talks failed when Guomindang troops attacked Communist troops elsewhere; the Republican-era buildings have been preserved as they were at the time.

In front of the complex there's a bronze statue of Zhou, his expression midway between serene and resolute. Inside, there are a number of displays. One details George Marshall's earlier attempts to moderate between the two parties in Chongqing. Others hold Zhou's leather jacket, his briefcase, his camera, his watch. The best exhibit consists of the beautiful black Buick that Zhou used while here in Nanjing.

Rain Flower Terrace Martyrs Museum

(雨花台烈士纪念馆)

The Rain Flower Terrace, previously mentioned in the context of the sixth-century Buddhist temples that once stood here, is also, sadly, focal to the twentieth-century history of Nanjing: it was the Guomindang's killing field from 1927 to 1949. The terrace is now a national park studded with memorials to the Communists who died here, and includes a large museum dedicated to that period. The gate is a massive concrete wall several meters thick. The monuments, mainly erected in the late 1980s, are built of beige stone and look like bunkers.

Among them is the Martyrs Monument: 42.3 meters tall for 4/23, April 23rd, the day in 1949 when the PLA entered Nanjing. The reflecting pool before the

monument is meant to symbolize blood. On the long walk up the several flights of stairs that lead to the foot of the monument, there are huge stone carvings of two songs in various languages, sheet music included: the "Internationale" and the national anthem of the People's Republic of China.

There is also a Group Statue, erected in 1979. The figures there stand in for the thousands who were brought here for execution in the course of those two decades.

The first section of the museum is mainly dedicated to telling individual stories briefly: a photograph, and then a paragraph of biography. Some of the leaders, of course, get their lives more fully told. The museum then tells its story of the development of the Communist party here in China. The exhibits are simple, repetitive and effective.

And there are descriptions of the many Communist plots and insurrections, most of which failed in those early days, nearly all ending in death for those that planned them. Alongside many of these placards are cases holding the martyrs' personal belongings: eyeglasses, an alarm clock, pen nibs, bamboo sewing needles.

Presidential Palace
(总统府)

The Presidential Palace rests on a site first used by the Ming, then by the Qing, briefly by the Heavenly Kingdom, and lastly by the Guomindang. Part of it has recently been remodeled to mimic what the Taiping built. The Throne Room has two very nice carved egrets to either side of a gold-plated throne. The Secret Room—Hong Xiuquan's study—has a fine Qing-era mahogany desk and a big blue bowl full of scrolls.

From there one enters the Guomindang section. It is mainly offices and meeting rooms which look exactly as you would expect them to look. Next is the Republican Museum, which attempts to sort out some of the spectacularly complicated history of that period, and has a fine collection of photographs, including one of government soldiers cutting the Manchu-style pigtails off the heads of some extremely discomfited civilians in the middle of the street as part of the campaign to "Abolish Feudal and Irrational Practices."

The other half of the grounds was once the site of the Heavenly King's mansion; now it consists of a large and very pleasant Ming-style garden known as Xuyuan, dotted here and there with Republican-era buildings. The Sun Yat-sen Office Building holds little of interest, though it does have an exhibit explaining that his government failed for only two reasons: lack of money, and lack of power.

His old residence is also here, as well as a pavilion, the Yilan Ge, which holds information on many of the main figures in the various Republican governments. Most interesting of the lot was a man by the name of Tang Xiangming, who was talented and flexible enough not only to survive but to thrive in positions of power through a tremendous range of governments over the course of five decades. Born in 1885, he made rank as a captain in the Manchu navy, then served as Vice Minister of the Navy under Sun Yat-sen, continued as a government official in the latter years of the Guomindang under Chiang Kai-shek, and then worked for the Communist party as well. He spent the last few years of his life studying Buddhism, and died in 1975 at the age of ninety.

Two other pavilions also bear mentioning. The first is notable mainly for its name: Wangfei Ge, the "Forgot to Fly Pavilion," was built in 1871, and is surrounded by scenery alleged to be so beautiful that birds forget to fly away. The other pavilion truly merits such a name, but is instead called the Mandarin Duck Pavilion. It was built by the Taiping, and has a double pinnacle, each peak with its own set of eaves, such that it appears to be two separate pavilions, one behind the other. This symbolized the Taiping belief, rare enough in its time, that men and women are equal.

煦園

John Rabe Residence

(约翰·拉贝故居)

The former residence of John Rabe, now formally and lengthily known as "The John Rabe and International Safety Zone Memorial Hall and John Rabe Research and Exchange Center for Peace and Reconciliation," contains only a limited amount of information not already found in Rabe's diaries, published in 1998 as *The Good Man of Nanjing*. That book is well worth reading, but for those who haven't had the opportunity, the exhibits here serve as an excellent introduction to what happened in Nanjing in the late 1930s, as experienced by this consistently noble, remarkably courageous, and slightly goofy Nazi official.

In 1937, as the Japanese troops drew near and news reached the city of the slaughters already carried out in Shanghai and elsewhere, Rabe helped to form the International Committee for the Nanjing Safety Zone, composed mainly of American doctors from Gulou Hospital and professors from Nanjing University, but also including several other foreign businessmen from Denmark and Great Britain. He was subsequently elected chairman of that committee.

When the city fell and the terror began, Rabe made use of his Nazi credentials to protect to the best of his abilities the thousands of Chinese who had evacuated to the ten square kilometers of the International Safety Zone, which was recognized (if not often respected) as neutral territory by the Japanese. He kept a series of journals documenting the horrific events he witnessed, and chose to remain in the city—against orders from his superiors at Siemens—until the worst of the Rape was over in late February of 1938.

Back in Berlin in 1941, Rabe spent a year copying out the 2100 pages he had compiled, documenting more than five hundred specific atrocities. However, after his first three weeks home he was no longer allowed to lecture on the material contained therein, nor to publish the diaries at any point—the Nazi government did not want to alienate its Japanese allies, and pressured Siemens (not that much pressure was needed) to prevent Rabe from working at their Berlin facility, or anywhere else for that matter.

Even in 1945, with Allied bombs exploding around him and conditions growing ever worse, he continued writing in his journals; the irony of his status as war victim on both sides of the conflict was not lost on him. By that point he had no way to sustain his wife and six children; the Nanjing City Assembly then collected two thousand

dollars to help him and his family. He died of a stroke in early 1950, and disappeared from history until 1996, when his granddaughter, Ursula Reinhardt, made his diaries public.

In the yard there is a reconstruction of the air-raid shelter Rabe himself dug, albeit not in its original location. It is a bit crypt-like: a hump of grass, and a hobbit-size arched door painted black and padlocked shut. There is also a bronze bust of Rabe, and the artist managed to capture him well—brave, intelligent, and strangely whimsical—but without the Nazi pin he utilized to save the lives of so many.

Republican-era Architecture

(民国建筑)

The final "site" worth mentioning is not a single location, but rather a series of small areas where Republican-era houses—many of them better described as mansions—can be seen. While the urge to modernize via destruction and reconstruction is a powerful force here as elsewhere, this form of architecture has a number of vocal supporters in Nanjing, and many of the houses have been main-

tained in excellent condition.

The best way to see these areas is on foot, particularly as many of the streets are pleasantly shaded with sycamores. The walk north along Ninghai Road from its intersection with West Beijing Road leads through an area rich in Republican architecture, much of it hidden away down the alleys to either side.

If one instead strikes out west from that same intersection, the walk will be a bit drab at first, but a right turn on Xikang Road will lead to the Xikang Hotel, which at one point housed the U.S. embassy; inside there are several fine wooden balconies still intact, and outside there's an old stone fountain built into a slightly labyrinthine, vine-covered entrance made of brick and stone. Finally, there is a long stretch of such structures on the forty-fourth block of West Beijing Road, and the Nanjing University campus, located at 22 Hankou Street, contains a great many beautiful buildings from this period.

Artifacts

In addition to the artifacts to be seen in the sites already mentioned, the Jiangsu Provincial Museum also has a few works of art from the Republican period. Of note for various reasons is an embroidery that Shen Shou copied from a Renaissance oil painting; it shows Christ wearing his crown of thorns, complete with Renaissance hair and a few discrete drops of blood. There are also modern red clay teapots in the form of persimmons, gourds and bamboo stalks. There is a fine ghostly painting of crabs by Qi Baishi, magpies on a willow by Xu Beihong, and a disquieting set of lotus paintings by Zhang Daqian. Lastly, there are calligraphic scrolls in forceful running script by Zhang Binglin, and one in the smooth running script of Shen Yinmo bearing a couplet—two lines of seven characters each—extracted from a poem by Du Zimei.

THE PEOPLE'S REPUBLIC OF CHINA

中华人民共和国

1949 – Present

Key Historical Figures: Mao Zedong (毛泽东)

Zhou Enlai (周恩来)

Historical Sites: First Nanjing Bridge (南京第一长江大桥)

毛 泽 东

Mao Zedong

Because Chiang Kai-shek and his government chose to flee rather than fight for Nanjing itself, the city was spared the absolute devastation wrought on so many other parts of the country toward the end of the Chinese civil war. That said, conditions here were still dire by most standards. The housing shortage was particularly acute: for the first few years after the PLA victory, the dorms and kitchens for college students (and for their professors as well) consisted of tents and camping equipment left behind by the puppet regime of Wang Jingwei that had ruled much of the country from Nanjing for the last several years of World War II. (Wang's tomb, originally located on Plum Blossom Hill, was demolished in 1946 to dishonor him for having collaborated with the Japanese invaders; it was replaced with a pavilion which is said to be the best place in Nanjing for observing plum trees in full bloom.)

After the establishment of the PRC and the return of the capital to Beijing, Nanjing once again found itself a regional rather than a national political center. While the party leadership in the north concerned itself with restructuring the government, curbing inflation, administering land reform and rooting out domestic opposition, Nanjing focused on getting back to the business of daily life.

Like much of the rest of the country, Nanjing threw itself enthusiastically into the Great Leap Forward, and suffered greatly, albeit less than poorer rural regions, from the horrific famine that followed. The city was hit again during the Cultural Revolution, when so many of its remaining historical relics were destroyed by the Red Guards, and so many of its intellectuals were sent to the countryside to be "reeducated." This latter period was particularly painful for Nanjing given that throughout its history it has more often been an intellectual and cultural capital than a political or military one.

All in all, the past few decades have not been unkind to Nanjing. The aftermath of student protests here dimmed local prospects for a time, but the local and regional governments have embraced Nanjing's status as a middle-sized city with an extraordinary richness of historical and artistic resources. Nanjing has invested heavily in the technological and service sectors, and in the tourism industry in particular. The city is once again prosperous, having risen above the violence of its history, and the outlook at present is bright.

First Nanjing Bridge
(南京第一长江大桥)

Of the sites from this period that might be of interest to visitors, the most significant by far is the First Nanjing Bridge. The bridge is perhaps less than elegant, but in part thanks to the bridgeheads, with their yellow towers topped with flag-shaped beacons, and their Socialist Realist statues—one in honor of those who built the bridge, the other beckoning to the rest of the world's socialists—it has a certain grim, broad-shouldered grace.

Begun in 1960 and finished in 1968, it has two decks—a four-lane road above and a two-track railway below—and each day it is crossed by some 50,000 cars and two hundred fifty trains. It is one of the longest bridges in China, stretching nearly 1600 meters from bank to bank, and almost five kilometers if one counts the approaches as well. It is held eighty meters above the bottom of the river by nine pillars that reach down through ten meters of empty space, thirty-five meters of water, and another thirty-five meters of silt and mud. The bridgehead towers are seventy meters tall, not counting the red steel flags that rise above them.

Work on the bridge began shortly after the Soviet engineers who had agreed to build it left in a politically-motivated huff, and after American engineers who had taken a look at the site declared the job impossible. In the words of Simon Winchester, "(The Americans) hadn't realized just who they were talking to. The China of the late 1950s was a country intoxicated with the madness of her Great Leap Forward, a people suffused with a barely rational pride and determination, and a nation whose technical institutes were filled with engineers who insisted they could manage the building of this bridge, however difficult, quite alone. It took them eight years, and it required the total reorganization of the Chinese steel industry to provide the necessary bars and girders. But they did it." And from that moment on, the Chinese believed themselves capable of anything.

One of the architects who helped to design the bridge still lives and works in Nanjing. Zhong Xunzheng first came to Nanjing in 1948, graduated from Southeast University (then called Central University) in 1952, and began working in its architecture department shortly thereafter. In 1958, he and his colleagues proposed a design for the bridgehead towers that was classically Chinese, with echoes of glories past, but the Ministry of Transport turned it down, then organized a competition, seeking a design for the towers that, in their words, "reflected the spirit of the era."

Zhong's new design for the towers was eventually chosen from among two hundred proposals. However, because of the famine that swept the country in the early 1960s, other projects took priority, and his plans were put aside. It was not until August of 1968—only two months before the bridge was scheduled to open—that his drawings were given the green light.

From beneath the bridge, if one looks landward and narrows one's field of vision, the view of the receding parallel lines of the immense columns gives the place an almost nave-like feel. There is the chorus of trains gunning back and forth on the tracks overhead, and of cars slipping across the roadway still higher. Staring up, one gets a clear sense of the massive industrial weight of the thing, the architectural stresses and strengths that keep it in the air.

Taking the elevator up to the level of the road and walking down the sidewalk into the whipping wind, there is another view, equally moving for some, of the shipyards to the east and the ferry stations to the west, of the river itself, and what it carries. The entire flotilla moves in slow motion from this distance. Immense barges are pulled upriver to offload their cargo: wheat, logs, iron. Much closer at hand, the guardrails are adorned with cast-iron sunflowers.

Up another level on the viewing platform, one is farther from the ships, but closer to the group statues and flags on the bridgehead. The statue on the south side of the bridge is led by two soldiers. One is a black man, dressed in a sort of robe, who

holds a large machine gun; the other is Chinese, bears an even larger machine gun and holds high his copy of *The Selected Works of Mao Zedong*. The statue on the north side has three figures marching proudly away from Nanjing: a soldier, a farmer, and a factory worker. There is also a young student, the only woman in the group, and she's facing the other direction, back toward the city.

LIVING CULTURE

OVERVIEW 总观

For reasons that will by now be clear, Nanjing has long been listed as one of the "Four Great Ancient Capitals of China" (along with Beijing, Luoyang and Xian, though in point of fact the official list has now expanded to eight, including Kaifeng, Hangzhou, Anyang, and Zhengzhou). However, over the course of the past five decades, the city has also built itself into a national powerhouse in terms of education and research, industry and transportation, and contemporary art and culture.

The climate in Nanjing is sub-tropical, with extremely hot summers, monsoons in winter, and a good deal of rain year-round. Given the proximity of the Yangtze River, Purple Mountain, and a number of small lakes, Nanjing's natural scenery is lovely. It also has several natural hot springs, including Tangquan Hot Spring in Pukou, and Tangshan Hot Spring in Jiangning.

The greater Nanjing area has a wealth of natural resources. While much of the city's job base and income continue to rely on the "Five Pillar Industries" developed in the first few decades of the People's Republic—electronics, motor vehicles, petrochemicals, iron and steel—it also produces computer software, textiles, and a variety of minerals including zinc and strontium. Also of note is the stoneware industry, which has combined Japanese technology with local ceramic clay and porcelain clay from other provinces to produce great varieties of dishware, as well as a majority of the world's ceramic exhaust filters.

While the city's legacy of state-owned enterprises still looms large, Nanjing has enjoyed a string of recent successes in attracting multinational firms: among others, Fiat, Sharp and Iveco have all established themselves here. This is in part a response to the city's investment in major industrial parks, of which it now has five.

Nanjing is also the main hub of transportation in eastern China. Expressways connect the city to Shanghai, Hefei and Hangzhou; the train system links Nanjing to the entire country as part of the Tianjin-Pukou line, with direct connections to Shanghai and Wuhu. Within the city, four bus companies cover 170 routes, and the metro system's second line will be completed by 2008. The airport handles both national and international travel, with flights to Japan, Korea and Thailand, among other foreign destinations, and is among China's top airports in terms of passenger and cargo traffic. Meanwhile, Nanjing's port is the largest in inland China: it is ninety-eight kilometers long, with sixty-four berths, sixteen of which serve ships over 10,000 tons, and the channel was recently deepened to ten-and-a-half meters, permitting the entrance of vessels of up to 50,000 tons at dead weight.

The city also excels in the area of higher education, and has done so since the forerunner of Nanjing University, then known as the Imperial Central College, was founded by the Eastern Wu in 258 A.D. As one of the four major scientific research centers in China, Nanjing is the site of some fifty universities and more than five hundred research institutes, with a city-wide total of 400,000 engineers, technicians and researchers. The Nanjing Library, established in 1907, is third-largest in the country, with more than seven million volumes; the Nanjing University Library, holding more than four million, is also a national research center. Of particular note is Nanjing University's partnership with Johns Hopkins University: together they have established the Hopkins-Nanjing Center, a world-famous facility for Chinese and American studies, with the only uncensored open-stacks library in China. Southeast University, the University of Aeronautics and Astronautics, Nanjing Forestry University, the University of Posts and Telecommunications, and the Nanjing Institute of Meteorology are also leaders in their fields.

Lastly, Nanjing now has fifteen sister cities around the world, including Florence, Leipzig, Perth, Nagoya, Eindhoven, Taejon, and two cities each in the United States (St. Louis and Houston) and France (Alsace and Hauts-de-Seine).

ART AND ARTISANSHIP
艺术和工艺

Art and Museums
(手工艺和博物馆地图)

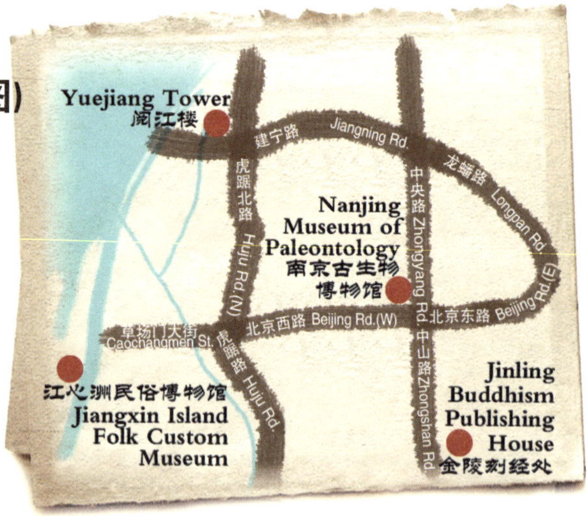

Introduction

(概况)

Much of Nanjing's historical presence is a function of the voices of its artists. As has been mentioned, the Wang-Xie Mansion remains standing on the strength of a single line by Tang poet Liu Yuxi, and seventeenth-century courtesan Li Xiangjun has been immortalized in a dozen different art forms; the poetry of Du Fu and Li Bai celebrate the city and its environs, and of China's four classic novels, three of them—*Dream of the Red Chamber, Outlaws of the Marsh,* and *Journey to the West*—have strong connections to Nanjing. Three thousand pieces of music have been written for the classical instrument known as the guqin; most of them were composed here, and almost a thousand have survived to the present day. In opera, in dance, in painting and photography, Nanjing has more often than not been the country's heart.

Moreover, the contemporary art scene in Nanjing stands toe-to-toe with that of any other Chinese city, Beijing included, in terms of the quality of the work being produced. Nanjing's historical reputation as a city that welcomes artists and their work—beginning as far back as the Liangzhu period 4500 years ago, and passing through the Eastern Jin, the Tang and the Song, straight through the Ming and the Qing—continues to draw writers, painters and musicians from the rest of southern China and beyond. The city's aura of culture past and present helps make it among the most pleasant places in China to live.

Contemporary Artists and Galleries (当代画家和美术馆)

In terms of painting, photography and installation art, two artists currently hold pride of place: Tang Guo's ink paintings of spirit stones appearing in dreams of old Nanjing, and Xu Lei's disquietingly planed views through modern doors and windows are sought by professional collectors the world over. Among younger artists, Sun Jianchun's lilies made of PLA uniforms, Chen Hui's gray abstracts suggesting history hidden by rain, and Gao Xiaojun's extraordinary oil paintings that appear to be photographs of faint ripples on dark water have all brought national acclaim.

These artists and others are supported by a strong cast of galleries, including the Jiangsu Art Gallery, the RCM Art Museum and Gallery, Jinling Stone Gallery, Square Gallery, and the Shenghua Art Center. The Jiangsu Art Gallery is the biggest and best established of this group, and has done good work in recent years with exhibitions from the New Jinling School.

Dance, Classical Music, Opera and Theater

(舞蹈，古典音乐，戏剧和剧院)

There are several worthy dance companies in Nanjing, including the Qianxian Dance Troupe, the Nanjing Dance Company, and the Arts Institute Experimental Dance Troupe. There is also an acrobatic company, two catch-all Art Troupes, and no fewer than eight orchestras, among them the Jiangsu Symphonic Orchestra, the Arts Institute Chinese Orchestra, and the Nanjing University of Science and Technology Wind Orchestra.

Moreover, a surprising number of venues, including the Jiangnan Theater, the Qianxian Theater and the Peking Opera Institute, offer different forms of stage performance, including spoken theater, puppet theater and a wide variety of operatic styles including Yang, Yue, Xi and Kun opera.

There are also several music schools dedicated to the tradition of music played on classical Chinese instruments. Ancient scholars were not considered worthy of the name unless they had mastered a musical instrument, and the guqin, with its twangy harmonics and smooth slides, was often thought to be the only acceptable choice. Cheng Gongliang, currently the finest guqin player in China, holds court and teaches class in the music department at the Nanjing Academy of Art. Meanwhile, at the Wang-Xie Mansion in the Confucius Temple district, the one room with air-conditioning is the stronghold of Gui Shimin, who likewise teaches the six hundred pieces of music written for the guqin that are still common currency in China.

As previously mentioned, the Gan Xi Residence has its own music school, which offers training on several classical instruments, including the guqin, the pipa and the erhu. It is also home to the local classical orchestra's practice sessions and concerts, and hosts weekly gatherings of Kun opera fans and amateur performers.

Kun Opera (昆曲)

Kun opera is both the oldest staged art form in China and the most significant art form to have originated in this region. Less shrill and percussive and more literary and dance-oriented than its (admittedly more famous) younger brother from Beijing, Kun opera began to develop more than five hundred years ago under the Ming dynasty, and reached its peak in popularity about two hundred years ago during the mid-Qing.

Since the early 1980s, the Jiangsu Province Kun Opera Theater has staged regular performances at its facility adjacent to Chaotian Palace. According to Vice-director Wang Bin, the company sees its primary mission as one of teaching contemporary audiences how to listen to this ancient art form with new ears. The company was founded in 1956 in Suzhou, performing a combination of Kun opera and Suzhou opera, but in 1960 the company split, and a new troupe was formed in Nanjing. From that point on, the Nanjing troupe has focused on what is considered the purest form of Kun opera.

In the course of the twentieth century, the entire art form very nearly disappeared on several different occasions. Battered by the chaos at the end of the Qing dynasty, it survived through the 1920s on the strength of a group of supporters who established an opera school in Suzhou and hired the last surviving Kun veterans to train up a new generation of actors.

In the 1940s, it was the turmoil of the Chinese civil war that threatened the existence of Kun opera: many troupes disbanded, and the actors scattered. However, in 1955 a new troupe was formed, and one night the following year, at the invitation of the government, they performed a famous opera called *Fifteen Strings of Coins*. Zhou Enlai and Mao Zedong were both in the audience that evening, and both praised the performance; as a result, various Kun troupes came in for state subsidies that were, by the standards of the time, quite generous.

With the founding of the Jiangsu Province Kun Opera Theater that same year, a new generation of actors was recruited—those who are now the elder performers on the stages of Nanjing and Suzhou. However, during the Cultural Revolution, Kun opera (along with most other traditional forms of drama) was banned for more than a decade. The actors continued to practice even as they labored in the fields, making notes of the lyrics they had memorized and hiding the scraps of paper away.

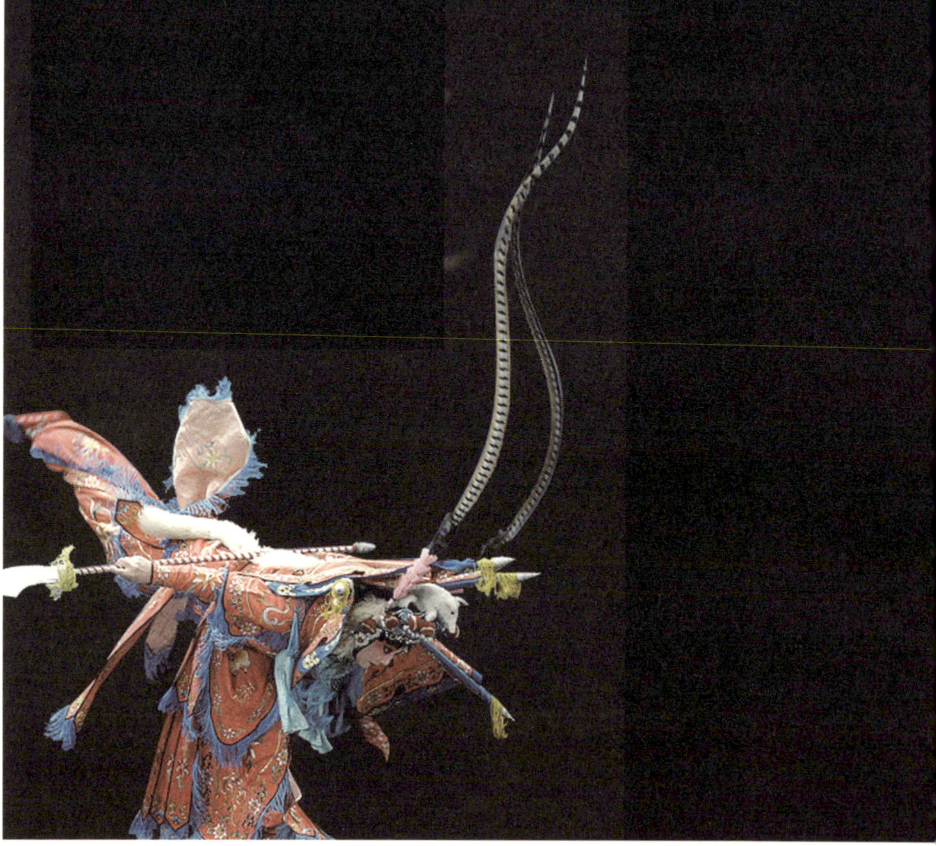

Since the end of the Cultural Revolution, two subsequent generations of actors have been trained up, the most recent graduating in 1998. Things now appear to be mainly back on track, with major troupes touring from their bases in Nanjing and six other major Chinese cities including Beijing, Shanghai and Suzhou.

However, Kun opera now faces another set of challenges. There is the predictable competition from cinema, television and other mediums, which draws both talent and support of all kinds away from older art forms. And in reaction to that competition, there is pressure—both from the cultural powers-that-be and from some directors as well—to modernize the form. They would prefer to see ever shorter productions staged in ever larger (and thus more lucrative) venues; this is a particular problem for art forms which, like Kun opera, were designed to unfold over a period of several days or even weeks, and to be performed in intimate settings for small numbers of spectators. The modernizers would also like to see new musical instruments added to the traditional orchestra, and further decoration and technology supplied to the originally bare Kun stage.

Resisting that pressure are purists who think that such changes are best left to Broadway. It would not be unprecedented for these two schools of thought—the purists and the modernists—to lead eventually to separate art forms, both of them competing for the Kun mantle. Whether or not this will actually occur remains to be seen.

Literature (文学)

The literary legacy of Nanjing is currently in good hands, as many of China's finest contemporary writers and poets call this city home. Perhaps the best known among them is Su Tong, author of *Wives and Concubines*, a collection of three novellas including the one on which the popular film *Raise the Red Lantern* was based. Among his subsequent books are the novels *Rice* and *My Life as Emperor*. Both *Wives and Concubines* and *Rice* are set in the China of the 1930s, but in each case the work takes what one thinks one knows of the past and makes it wholly other, using deliberately complex shifts in time, oracular pronouncements by unnamed first-person narrators, and styles of diction that are new to this earth. The author's forward to *My Life as Emperor* states that the book is meant to be bound by neither historical time nor literal place, but careful readers will note significant parallels between the fictional Xie empire and many of the signature moments in Chinese history, both ancient and modern.

Su Tong
(苏童)

Ye Zhaoyan has long been among the most popular and prolific writers in contemporary China. The son of Ye Shaojun, one of the most important Chinese writers of the 20th century, Ye Zhaoyan has won most of the major prizes and awards that China has to offer, but it was not until the recent publication of *Nanjing 1937: A Love Story* that he became better known abroad. His first five novels include *Dead Water*, *The Red House Restaurant*, and *Approaching the Evening*, all of which were highly experimental in nature; for *Nanjing 1937* he turned to a quieter realism to tell the story of a self-centered univer-

Ye Zhaoya（叶兆言）

sity professor whose attempt at love is intertwined with the appalling historical reality of the Japanese invasion of the city. Ye has also published a great deal of nonfiction, mainly focusing on the history of Nanjing, with essay collections including *Old Nanjing* and *Parking the Boat on the Qinhuai River*.

Despite his relatively young age, the poet, essayist and critic Han Dong has long held court in the cafes and bars of Nanjing. He is one of the Third Generation poets who write partly in reaction to the idealistic tones of the previous generation of “Misty” poets, while simultaneously acknowledging their debt to those poets for having forged several new kinds of experimental space and diction. Han and his fellow Third Generation poets have at times found great (even necessary) value in opacity and language games, and have little use for attempts at collective meaning, grandiose ideals, or writing framed to appeal to the economic, political or cultural powers that be. A certain amount of Han Dong’s work can be found in English, including a number of poems ably translated by the American poet Donald Revell.

Other major Nanjing writers include Bi Feiyu, much of whose work has been translated into French, though only anthologized stories have thus far made it into English; fiction writers and poets Lu Yang and Gu Qian; and Zhu Wen, a short story writer and filmmaker currently based in Beijing, whose collection *I Love Dollars* was recently translated by Julia Lovell.

Artisanship and Folk Arts
(工艺和民间艺术)

Goldfoil
(金箔)

The process of coating objects with infinitesimally thin sheets of gold has nearly two millennia of history in this area. Goldfoil was originally used mainly for the decoration of Buddhist statues; the tradition of wrapping food and medicine in goldfoil as an elixir began 300 years ago, and continues to this day. Under the Qing, gold thread was also needed to form royal silk brocade. Goldfoil is now used to adorn statues, furniture, screens, vases, tableware and bookplates, as well as purely decorative objects such as framed pictures and couplets. It has also been used to decorate whole cupolas and other architectural features at, among other places, the Zairian Presidential Palace in Kinshasa, the Beijing Hotel in Moscow, Tiananmen Tower, Potala Palace, and the Shaolin Temple.

Silk Brocade
(云锦)

The Nanjing Brocade Museum houses a brocade workshop and a research institute where one can see the roots and current production of perhaps the most fascinating of Chinese textile arts. Nanjing brocade, also known as cloud brocade, is one of three ancient styles (the others being the Shu and the Song) which together boast nearly 1500 years of historical use. The form of zhuang hua loom on which Nanjing brocade is woven was first invented more than 4700 years ago.

The central mission of the textile scientists and historians at the research institute is to join archaeologists wherever fragments of ancient silk have been found, to bring samples back here and analyze them, and if possible to reproduce them. The work involved in that latter step alone is immense: it took the institute thirteen years to discover the techniques necessary to recreate the velvet-loop brocade found in a Han dynasty tomb. The result is a swath of silk so thin that it is transparent enough to read through, and so light that the entire bolt, all seventeen meters of cloth, can be folded to fit in the palm of one's hand.

The museum has displays of many of the historical garments reconstructed here, including Ming warrior uniforms and Dragon Robes, as well as a number of robes worn by civil servants. Each of these robes bears its bu, the imperial insignia that announces the rank of its wearer. The robes of civil officials were generally decorated with images of birds, with the beautiful "Number One Rank Crane Insignia" used for those of the highest rank; robes intended for military officers instead bore animals such as the lion, tiger, jaguar or horse.

The facility also organizes a daily fashion show, with predictably tall and attractive young women modeling garments made and sold here, many of them designed along the lines of ancient fabrics and patterns.

Silk Lanterns
(绸灯)

Near the Confucius Temple, there is a family-owned workshop dedicated to the craft of making the lanterns used in all major Chinese festivals, and in various other types of display. The Gu family has been producing these lanterns at what is now known as the Art Center of Handicraft Lanterns for more than fifty years. Their home's central courtyard is surrounded by old brick buildings filled both with new lanterns recently ordered and yet to be picked up, and with old lanterns kept as display models for prospective customers.

The biggest lanterns take two weeks to make, and sell for a few hundred dollars. The process of building them involves welding heavy metal bases to fit the lanterns that have been ordered; adding the wire frames; wiring in the light bulbs, which may number in the hundreds for a big lantern; stretching the cloth background—a blend of silk and polyester—over the frame and gluing it in place; and finally adding the decorative fabrics and other elements needed to bring the lantern to life, including eyes, scales, and auspicious Chinese characters. The colors on the new lanterns are typically very bright: orange, red, green, blue, and above all, gold.

The family's busy season is, naturally, right before the Lantern Festival, but they also produce work for most other holidays, and for Kun opera troupes and television shows. Each Lantern Festival, they sell a few hundred of the small square or octagonal palace lanterns known as gong deng; the fatter, rounder lanterns called deng long (the name derived from that of the bamboo steamers used to make dim sum) are most popular around National Day.

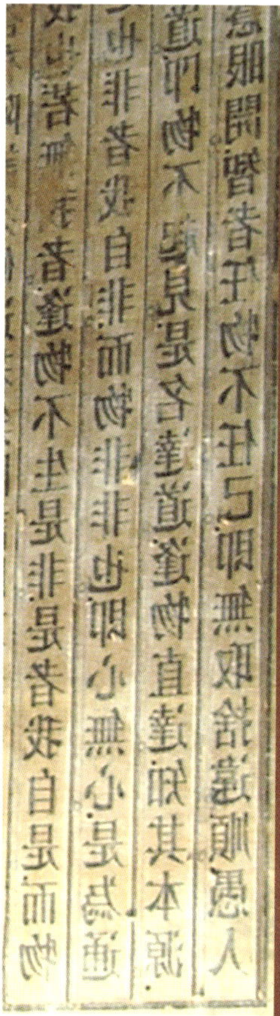

Jinling Buddhism Publishing House

(金陵刻经处)

Though it can only be visited by special appointment, the Jinling Buddhism Publishing House is a fascinating facility dedicated to Buddhist theological research, and to the printing of Buddhist texts using hand-carved wooden plates. It was established by Yang Renshan, who was born in Anhui province in 1839; following in his father's footsteps, he became an officer in the Qing army, and joined his father in the war against the Taiping.

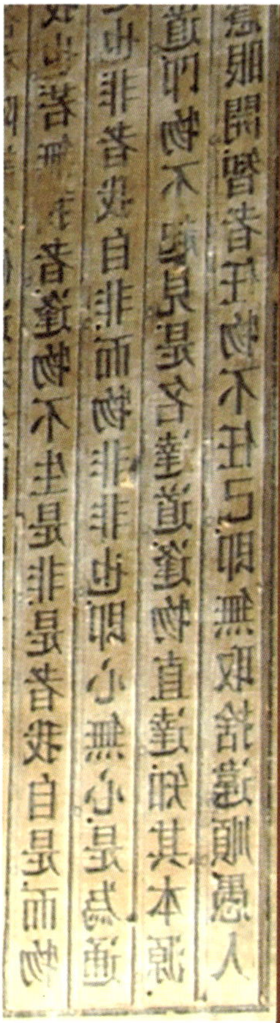

Yang stayed in Nanjing after the rebellion had been put down, dedicated himself to the study of Buddhism, and two years later he pooled his resources with those of ten other laymen to found this house. There is now an on-site museum with information about Yang's life, and about the history of the printing house; it also holds copies of many of the texts produced under his supervision. Of perhaps greater interest is the library next door. In addition to the first plate ever carved here—the frontispiece of "The Most Excellent Four Books on this Pure Earth"—the stacks contain a total of 130,000 block sutras, of which 47,000 were made here. The plates are black with age and use, and many need repairs before they can be used again. It is the biggest collection of its kind in the world.

This is one of only two such printing houses in China; the other is in Hangzhou, and deals mainly with classical works of literature. Here, projects in both Chinese and Japanese are accepted, and clients aren't charged for the carving of the plates, only for the ink and paper used in printing. Moreover,

the house recently augmented its production capability by adding a wing holding advanced printing facilities. The computerized press handles mainly new texts, while reproductions of ancient texts continue to be printed from hand-carved plates as they have been for thousands of years.

Museums and Artifacts

(博物馆和工艺品)

Nanjing is blessed with more than seventy museums, including some of the oldest and best in the country. In addition to the Jiangsu Provincial Museum and the others named thus far, there are museums dedicated to specific historical periods and to various scientific fields, among a great many other cultural spheres.

Nanjing Museum of Paleontology

(南京古生物博物馆)

The Nanjing Museum of Paleontology, administered by the Chinese Academy of Sciences, specializes in invertebrate paleontology, micropaleontology, and paleobotany. It has a good copy of the homo erectus skull found in the cave at Leigong, and a number of fine dinosaur skeletons. However, its central display focuses on the extraordinary discovery made at Chengjiang in 1984: a massive cache of early Cambrian fossils. The discovery's importance stems not just from the age of the fossils—approximately 530 million years old—but from the light they shed on the evolutionary history of life: the Chengjiang trove is one of very few in the world to include soft-bodied marine animals.

Elsewhere there are four other large displays, one each dedicated to the Precambrian, Paleozoic, Mesozoic and Cenozoic periods. There are also fifteen smaller exhibits, including Oceans of the Dinosaur Era, and Paleobotanic Garden. Finally, there is a display regarding the incredibly diverse flora and fauna of the Jehol area, which includes the lake shales at Jingangshan in Liaoning Province to the northeast. While perhaps better known to paleontologists than to the general population, the Jehol region has produced a number of fossils which together have rewritten paleontological history, including that of the feathered dinosaur known as Sinosauropteryx.

Jiangxin Island Folk Custom Museums

(江心洲民俗博物馆)

Out on Jiangxin Island, which can be reached via ferry from the dock at the end of Dinghuaimen Road, there is a series of folk custom museums, all of which bear the unfortunate moniker “Happily Farmhouse” and tend toward the kitsch, but are worth visiting for several reasons.

The main museum, known as the All Trades Hall, contains exhibits on more than a hundred local trades, including plowing and planting, carding and weaving, fishing both with nets and with cormorants, embroidery and pottery and blacksmithing. While the painted plaster human figures here and in the other parts of the museum are perhaps not worth lingering over, and while the placards are often incomprehensible, there is a wealth of antique tools and implements including beautiful old spindles and looms, massive ceramic pots, and a terrific old bean-curd wheel made of stone. Furthermore, the walls of many of the displays are lined with superb photographs from the 1920s, ‘30s and ‘40s.

Meanwhile, at the nearby Agricultural Tools Museum, there is an antique rice thresher, a foot-powered water pump, a peanut sheller and a rice puffer, a vicious-looking rice plow and a century-old hand-powered fire hydrant that can still shoot a steady stream of water more than sixty meters.

Yuejiang Tower

(阅江楼)

The Yuejiang Tower stands at the top of Lion Hill in the northwest part of the city. It was built in 2001, but in a sense it is much older: the first Ming emperor designed it, and intended to build it, but the imperial treasury ran dry before he managed to start. A series of other emperors also announced plans to built it, but somehow it never got done until the Xiaguan District government stepped in.

The first floor has a display dedicated to Hongwu's belongings, including a beautiful rosewood replica of his Dragon Throne. One of the inscriptions bears his motto: "The boat floating on the water." By this he meant to remind himself that much as the water will support a sea-worthy craft, the people will support a just emperor, and much as waves can overturn a boat, so too can the people rise up against their rulers. There's also a good history display with information about each of the Ming emperors, including both highlights and lowlights, the latter best illustrated by the brief discussion of the sixteenth emperor, Xizong: "He was muddleheaded for all his life, and villains controlled the government."

On the second floor there is a display of other Ming artifacts, and a series of excellent exhibits on various luminaries who came to prominence during the Ming dynasty, including scientists such as Li Shizhen and Xu Guangqi, writers such as Wu Cheng'en (*Journey to the West*) and Luo Guanzhong (*The Romance of the Three Kingdoms*), and painters and calligraphers including Tang Yin and Zhou Chen. (There is also a shop selling modern calligraphy, as well as caricatures of the Buddha, Yasser Arafat and Richard Nixon painted on small rocks.)

The third floor holds a good exhibit on Zheng He, with large, well-made models of his ships, and a fair amount of information about his voyages. The fourth has handicrafts for sale, the fifth a teahouse. The sixth floor gets one closest to the ceiling, which features an immense gilded dragon; all told, more than eleven kilograms of gold were needed for the gilding done here at the tower. This final floor also has an outer balcony providing excellent views of the Yangtze River to the west, the factories and smokestacks to the northwest, the shipyards to the northeast, and the whole great stretch of central Nanjing to the south and southwest.

Folk Art and Artifacts
(民间艺术和文物)

The Jiangsu Provincial Museum has a large room dedicated to folk art, which, like most such work, walks carefully down the line between the utilitarian and the decorative. Many of the items on display pertain to religious and cultural holidays as celebrated in the countryside, which in turn are often determined by the changing seasons, and by the agricultural and other activities common to each season.

Some of the most beautiful pieces here are block prints, including a wonderful "Kindly Madam" print used for Spring Festival, and another showing fifteen women dressed as generals, which is taken from the Song dynasty story of the women of the Yang family, who took it upon themselves to defend the country when their husbands had all been killed on the battlefield. There are also paper cuttings used to decorate silk or bronze festival ornaments, one of which illustrates in great detail a scene from the classic drama *Romance of the West Chamber*, written by Yuan dynasty playwright Wang Shipu. Additionally there are silk flowers, masks meant to ward off evil, kites and banners and musical instruments, fans and goblets and a magnificent sedan chair in red and gray silk with brocade borders, topped with an Immortal riding a bixie made of blue and gray beads.

Meanwhile, in the folk art section of the Gan Xi Residence Museum, there are rooms dedicated to painting, music, calligraphy, paper cuttings, seals and stamps, shadow puppets, children's toy tops, and masks. The house offers courses in the production of all of these items, as well as seminars on how to stage one's own shadow-plays.

SCIENCE, NATURE, AND GREEN SPACES
科学，自然和绿色自然空间

Outside the City
(郊区地图)

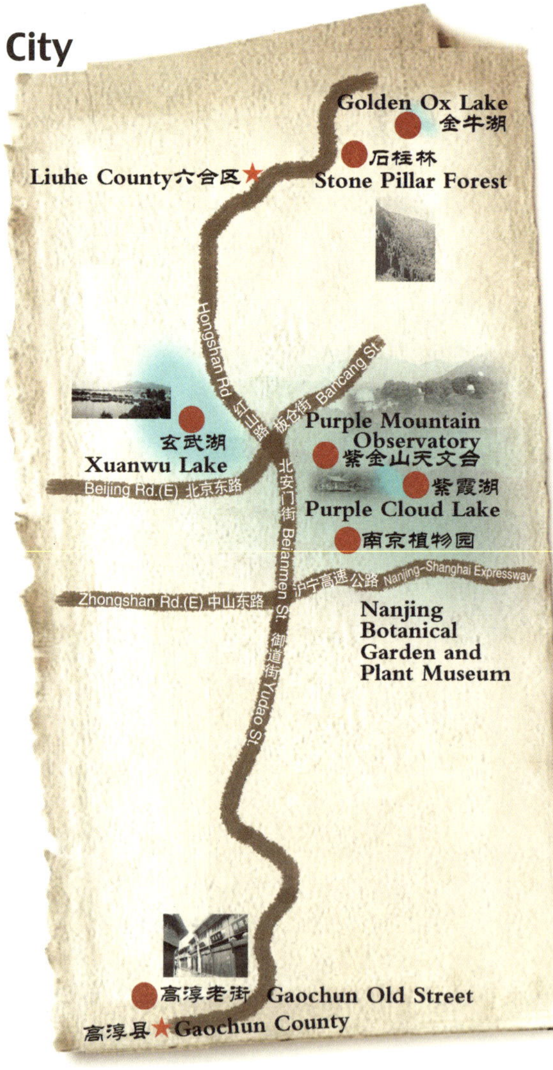

Purple Mountain Observatory
(紫金山天文台)

The domed telescopes of the Purple Mountain Observatory have facilitated a number of discoveries, among them three comets and some one hundred forty-seven asteroids, all of which were discovered between 1955 and 1983 under the supervision of its longtime director, Zhang Yuzhe. Of perhaps greater interest to the casual visitor are the splendid views of the valley that can be had from its heights, and the collection of ancient astronomical equipment gathered in its central gardens. Most of these pieces were stolen by the Eight Allied Powers in 1900, and returned to China after negotiations with Chiang Kai-shek in 1920.

There is an armillary sphere cast in 1427 under the Ming, and constructed along lines similar to those of the sphere invented by Western Han astronomer Luo Xinhong in 104 B.C. It is decorated with fine bronze dragons, and the mechanism itself consists of three nested rings used to measure the equatorial elliptic and horizontal coordinates of celestial bodies.

There is also a theodolite for measuring the horizontal coordinates of stars, and a gnomon of the sort first developed here in China three thousand years ago, used to obtain the exact dates of the summer and winter solstices, and the precise length of the tropical year. However, the most beautiful of the instruments here may be the abridged armilla, a Yuan dynasty improvement on the armillary sphere; its canted, interconnecting wheels are adorned with dragons and engraved with cloud symbols. The abridged armilla was invented by Guo Shoujing, and is capable of calculating the equatorial and horizontal coordinates of stars simultaneously.

City Parks and Gardens
(公园)

One of the most significant measures of the quality of life in Nanjing is the city's great number of trees, parks, and botanical gardens. From the sycamores that line so many of its avenues, to the massive gardens around a number of its historical monuments, to the natural areas outside of the city and the literally dozens of small parks that dot the space within its walls, Nanjing possesses more green spaces than most cities its size, and is justifiably proud of them.

Li Shizhen
李时珍

Nanjing Botanical Garden and Plant Museum
(南京植物园和植物博物馆)

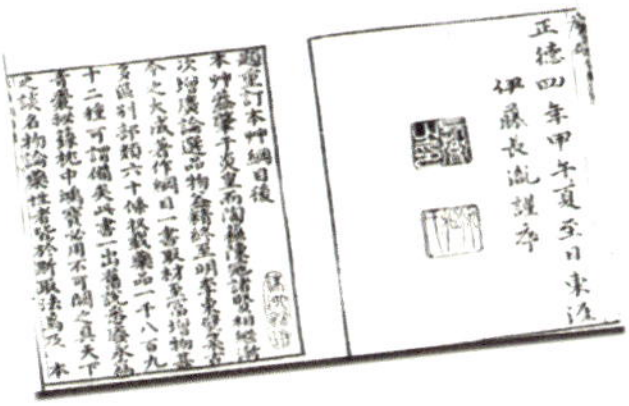

The Nanjing Botanical Garden and Plant Museum lies near the bottom of the southwest slope of Purple Mountain. It covers one hundred eighty-six hectares and contains more than 3000 plant species. It is as beautiful as such places tend to be, and perhaps the most popular site in Nanjing for couples getting their wedding pictures taken.

Near the entrance there is a statue of Li Shizhen, the Ming dynasty botanist and pharmacologist considered to be the founder of Chinese herbal medicine. Considered China's greatest naturalist, he analyzed more than 1000 different species, mainly by ingesting them and cataloguing the effects they had on his body. He was indebted to Zheng He for a great number of plants brought back from abroad; it is said that the great navigator even helped Li in organizing his classificatory structure. Li's masterwork, the *Compendium of Materia Medica*, was the result of more than forty years of research into the vast array of herbal lore at his disposal.

Purple Cloud Lake (紫霞湖)

Purple Cloud Lake, located just northeast of the Xiaoling Tomb on Purple Mountain, is a popular escape from the summer heat.

The lake covers an area of 45,000 square meters, and is said to have begun its life as an immense bomb crater created during the war against the Japanese. The administrators at the Sun Yat-sen mausoleum then decided to dam its outflow to store drinking water. Surrounded by pines and maples, it is one of the most pleasant areas near the city.

Xuanwu Lake
(玄武湖)

玄武湖

The islands of Xuanwu Lake have already been mentioned in the context of the tax and census archives kept there under the Ming. However, they also bear mentioning for their collection of parks and gardens.

All of the islands are well forested and nicely landscaped. The main entrance to the southwest leads in along a dike to Ring Island. This island is covered with camphor and French parasol trees, and has a large lotus-filled cove where a statue of the Lotus Fairy stands; she looks rather in a hurry for some reason, and is surrounded by four fat Lotus Angels who do not. Known as Lotus Square, this is the location of nightly summer shows integrating fountains, music, lasers and water-screen movies.

玄武湖

Farthest north is Liang Island, also known as America. (Each island has two names, one of which is taken from a given continent; in general they are better known by their non-continental names.) Here is where the bulk of the archives were kept; there is also a Friendship Hall, a Peony Garden, the Bronze Hook Well, a rather chaotic Bonsai Garden, the Hear Cock Crow Pavilion, the Lake God Temple, the Sightseeing Building and the Fish-Watching Pool.

Green Island to the northeast has a fine collection of tree gardens, including pines, cedars, willows and bamboo. Lastly, Water Chestnut Island to the southeast is famous for the thick mists that swirl down from Purple Mountain to engulf it. It also holds the largest aviary in China, with two hundred species and a total of more than 10,000 birds. Built in front of the aviary is an immense plant sculpture of two dragons fighting over a monstrously large flaming pearl.

玄武湖

For a more complete sense of the ways in which this city combines the aesthetic pleasures of water, wood, stone and mountain, and for a better look at many of Nanjing's smaller parks, consider striking out on foot. One good walk heads east from the Stone City Culture Area on the banks of the Outer Qinhuai, taking in Qingliang Hill, Wulong Pond Garden and Guofang Garden along the way, then turns north-northwest, passing through the elegant campus of Nanjing Normal University, the Yanlugong Ancestral Hall, and the National Defense Garden, before arriving at the Gulin Park area that surrounds the Jiangsu Television Tower.

Outside the City
(南京郊区)

In addition to the many previously discussed sites outside the city limits, there are a number of other locations worth seeing. Across the Yangtze are both Gaochun County southwest of Nanjing, and Liuhe County to the northwest. These two regions offer an interesting blend of the historical and the natural, and make for worthwhile day trips if one's schedule permits.

Gaochun County
(高淳县)

Gaochun County has several small sites of interest, including a number of agricultural and ecological tour zones set up along Gaochun and Gucheng Lakes, as well as in the town of Yaxi at the base of Youzi Mountain. The Zhenru Temple on the south slope of Youzi is also worth a look for its Buddha statue measuring twenty-one meters tall and weighing some three hundred tons. The area is dotted with crab farms, and celebrates Hairy Crab Festival each September. However, the area most worth visiting lies in the town of Gaochun itself, and is known simply as Old Street.

Gaochun Old Street

(高淳老街)

Gaochun has been a commercial center for the region since the fifth century A.D. There were some two hundred stores on Old Street as of the early years of the Qing dynasty; the majority of the buildings stood two stories tall, with one or two showrooms facing the street, and a number of other rooms—a workshop, a sitting room, a counting room and bedrooms—built toward the rear. The upstairs areas were generally used as storage, and there were horse-head firewalls built between the residences.

The street runs some eight hundred meters east to west; it was originally very narrow in spots, but has recently been widened to an average of five meters. Many of the doors, balustrades and doorposts are decorated with beautiful wood carvings, including images of lions, dragons, and local historical figures. The eaves of the buildings are conjoined all along the street, forming a corridor that gives the area a certain feeling of intimacy.

There are many small alleys leading off the main street. Temples adorned with figures of the Immortals were built on many of the street-corners, though they have nearly all been adopted for other uses. However, a number of Ming- and Qing-era storefronts have been restored, which is the main reason why the street has often been used as the setting for Chinese movies and television series, including "The Battle of Huangqiao," "The Water Margin, " and "Zhang Wenxiang Stabs a Horse."

A few of the addresses on this street bear special mention. At No. 13 is the Gaochun Brick and Stone Carving Museum, which has a large collection of portrait bricks dating back to the first century A.D., and a number of more recent stone carvings. At No. 93 is the former headquarters of the PLA's Fourth Army. This building was originally the central hall of the Wu family residence, built toward the end of the Ming dynasty. It contains an amphitheater with room for a thousand people, and two exhibition areas.

These historical sites aside, this still-vibrant market street is much like any other in China, with goods spilling out of the storefronts onto the sidewalks. Most common are the small seafood markets: men and women sitting in front of plastic tubs filled with live oysters, crabs, crayfish, shrimp and various species of fish. There are also a number of stores selling cloth shoes, several traditional pharmacies, and half a dozen shops that sell goose-feather fans. The biggest

福壽齊来合家歡
錢財廣進滿堂樂

fans are half a meter in diameter, and almost perfectly round. They come dyed in many colors, and some also bear peacock, pheasant or hawk feathers, but the most beautiful fans are sheer white, like immense opalescent seashells.

Liuhe County （六合区）

Driving through the open fields of Liuhe County, it is easy to see how the lilting, sylvan, omnipresent melody of the famous Chinese folk song "Hao Yiduo Molihua" ("A Beautiful Jasmine Flower") came to be written here. Among the sites worth seeing is the Liuhe Confucius Temple; dating back to the Tang dynasty, it is one of the oldest Confucian temples in the country. Also of note are the exhibits of folk art that take place in many of the local villages. Some of this work has been shown as far away as the Netherlands, and the rough lines and beautiful colors are a fine introduction to a certain view of life here. In these same towns, Rain Flower Pebbles can be found nearly everywhere; the agate is in fact gathered here rather than on the Rain Flower Terrace closer to Nanjing.

Golden Ox Lake (金牛湖)

Golden Ox Lake, located at the foot of Jinniu Mountain, is the largest artificial lake in the Nanjing area, covering a total of one hundred twenty-four square kilometers. The Dragon Boat races are often held here during the festival of the same name. Only twenty meters deep in the center, the lake has a large leisure area where bicycles, pedal-boats and motorboats can be rented; tour boats leave hourly from the main dock.

Stone Pillar Forest （石柱林）

By far the most significant point of interest in Liuhe County is the Stone Pillar Forest on Matou Hill. The forest is a type of geological formation that has only been found at four sites on earth, of which this is the biggest. Massive gray pentagonal and hexagonal stone columns line the inside of the hill's shell, of which some four-fifths survives; the area inside the hill covers nearly a fifth of a square kilometer, and the hill itself is about fifty meters tall. The columns are fifteen percent iron by volume, but also contain traces of gold, bronze, and other metals. They measure approximately half a meter on each side, and rise twenty to thirty meters up from the soil, with another two hundred meters hidden below ground.

The farther the pillars stand from the hill's shell, the shorter they are, resulting in a visual effect that is indeed much like that of a forest covering a steep downward slope. Some of the pillars are tall and straight, others are grouped together in formations resembling waterfalls, while still others radiate to the sides like fireworks. This last-named formation is in some ways the most relevant, given that actual fireworks are constantly being set off at the base of the forest. The people lighting the fuses are mainly Chinese senior citizens who have come here as members of tour groups, and because of the hollowed-out shape of the hill, the explosions echo on and on and on.

CUISINE 美食

食

Nanjing's cuisine owes a great deal to the city's proximity to the Yangtze River, and to the fish and shellfish farms spread out across the lakes and ponds of neighboring counties. For this reason, several of the most famous local delicacies involve crabs and crayfish, often torn apart by hand. (The visitor's hand, that is. Many restaurants provide not only bibs but elbow-length plastic gloves, and bowls of cilantro floating in water with which to scrub your hands afterward.) In the fall, when the hairy crabs have grown to edible size, they are readily available throughout Nanjing; among the most popular dishes are crab-and-pork dumplings, both for their delicious taste and because they require rather less effort than the steamed crabs also on the menu.

Other seafood dishes popular here include squid in pepper sauce, and yellow shrimp with bean curd. As for fish, there is eel in soy sauce or with mushrooms, silver carp servėd whole, mandarin fish in soy sauce and rice wine, and spicy tofu served with strips of freshwater shark.

Salted pressed duck is a regional specialty, as are duck kidneys with garlic, and duck-meat dumplings; chicken of course comes in hundreds of forms, the meat most commonly served in pepper sauce or diced with peanuts, and the feet served cold. The eggs too come in many ways, but the two most common are thousand-year eggs and, for those who don't have that kind of time, Living Pearl Eggs. The latter have been fertilized and allowed to mature for eight to twelve days; the juice is sucked out through a hole poked in one end of the shell, and the embryo is then tweezed out with chopsticks and eaten.

Among the favored local cooked vegetables are fried lotus root patties, steamed taro, lotus root in sweet sauce, and a number of vegetables grown only here in the region, the most common of which tastes like anise and is generally served with strips of dry tofu. Local salads include the marinated strips of potato and bell pepper also common elsewhere; additionally there are salads made of chrysanthemum leaves, water chestnuts, celery and lily root, baby lotus stalks, fresh lotus root, and the perennial favorite, carrot and pig's ear.

There are of course also restaurants serving food from many other areas of China, including Xinjiang, Sichuan, Guangdong, Hunan, and Henan, not to mention hotpot and dumplings. And there are many restaurants serving the food of other nations; Nanjing is particularly strong in terms of Korean and Japanese cuisine, but there are also Mexican, Italian, Brazilian, Thai, American and Indian restaurants, among others.

Many of Nanjing's best Chinese and international restaurants (as well as dozens of bars and teahouses) are located on Shiziqiao, an offshoot of Hunan Road, near the thirty-meter-long neon tube known as the Light Tunnel. Great street-food can be had in the Qingdao Lu area, and there are both high- and low-end restaurants in Xinjiekou near the city center. Other options include the 1912 area described in further detail below, the Xinleyuan area near the Nanjing Sheraton, and the large tourist area surrounding the Confucius Temple.

食

ENTERTAINMENT
娱乐

Festivals (节庆)

This region has always been home to dozens of different festivals: past traditions included climbing the city wall in January, swimming in Qingxi in March, and hiking the surrounding hills in September. While these and other festivals have mostly fallen by the wayside, new ones have sprung up to take their places.

福

The International Plum Blossom Festival, held each March on Plum Hill, brings in thousands of domestic and international tourists. The Lantern Festival lights up the Confucius Temple area on the fifteenth day of the first lunar month, which can fall in February or March of the Gregorian calendar. Outside the city, there are the Peach Blossom and Kite Festivals on Bagua Island, the Grape Festival on Jiangxin Island, and the Linggu Temple Sweet Osmanthus Festival on Purple Mountain.

Other festivals previously mentioned include the Dragon Boat Festival at Golden Ox Lake in April, the Chrysanthemum Festival at Xuanwu Lake in August, and the Hairy Crab Festival in Gaochun in September.

小吃

Nightlife (夜生活)

For more than a millenium, Nanjing's nightlife was centered around the Confucius Temple area, and elsewhere along the banks of the Qinhuai River. Now, however, things have decentralized a bit. The recently opened 1912 complex near the Presidential Palace has several dozen restaurants, bars, pubs, tea houses, nightclubs and discos.

The buildings are all Republican-era strucures: Large, squarish brick buildings not without charm, featuring four-sided roofs and protruding bay windows. The vast majority of them have been gutted and the establishments mentioned above then built inside, though towards the back there are still a few buildings housing Chinese residents who have thus far resisted the local efforts at gentrification.

Shopping

(购物)

For real antiques, the best place to go is Jubao Zhai Antiques, a government-run facility that carries old ceramics, carvings, porcelain, paintings and scrolls. If you're less concerned as to whether what you've bought is really as old as you'd like to think, the flea market at Chaotian Palace is a good place to spend an afternoon, discovering beautiful oddities that seem hardly to have a place in the world any more, and small tools meant for tasks that no longer need performing. There are bits of jade, small marble carvings, chops in all sizes and colors, prayer beads and urns and ashtrays, and a great variety of inexplicable chintz including ceramic soccer balls and roosters.

For quality handcrafts, the Nanjing Handcraft Center has a good selection of work in jade, silk embroidery, fans, lacquer ware and jewelry. There are also the gift shops at the Jinling Hotel, the Sheraton and the Hilton, which sell high-priced but genuine porcelain and crystal, as well as antiques and curios. Finally, silk brocade is best bought at the Nanjing Brocade Museum and Research Institute, though the quality there does not come cheap.

For souvenirs, the first place to check is the maze of streets around the Confucius Temple. Here you will find Rain Flower pebbles (both of genuine agate and of acrylic), cheap folding fans and wood carvings, jade and calligraphy, along with a great many other types of trinkets. Rain Flower pebbles can also be found on Rain Flower Terrace itself, and very nearly everywhere else in the city that tourists might possibly go.

Finally, just north of Bailu Zhou Park there's a very nice little market selling plants and fish and birds and pet insects. Even if you don't need any of those things, spending time there is as useful as a massage in terms of lowering your blood pressure.

Listings (列表)

Art Galleries and Troupes 美术馆和艺术团

Jiangsu Art Gallery
江苏省美术馆
Jiangshusheng Meishu Guan
地址：长江路 266 号
电话：025-8450 6789

RCM Art Museum and Gallery
RCM 艺术博物馆
RCM Yishu Bowuguan
地址：北京西路 72 号 1 楼
电话：025-8322 3399

Nanjing Little Red Flower Art Ensemble
南京小红花艺术团
Nanjing Xiaohonghua Yishutuan
地址：中山北路 148 号
电话：025-8322 9601

Cinemas 电影院

Nanjing Arts and Culture Center
南京文化艺术中心
Nanjing wenhua yishu zhongxin
地址：长江路 101 号
电话：025-8479 7961

影视百花园
Yingshi Baihuayuan
地址：延龄巷 115 号
电话：025-8664 6996

和平电影院
Heping Dianyingyuan
地址：中山北路 110 号
电话：025-8322 4134

大华电影院
Dahua Dianyingyuan
地址：中山南路 67 号
电话：025-8472 1634

Cultural Sites 文化景点

Art Center of Handicraft Lanterns
彩灯工艺厂
Caideng Gongyi Chang
地址：剪子巷路 84 号
电话：136-0515-2205

Jinling Buddhism Publishing House
金陵刻经处
Jinling KejingChu
地址：淮海路 35 号
电话：025-8454 2531

Purple Mountain Observatory
紫金山天文台
Zijinshan Tianwen Tai
地址：钟山第三峰天堡山
电话：025-8443 2310

Silk Brocade Research Institute
云锦研究所 Yunjin Yanjiusuo
地址：茶亭东街 240 号
电话：025-8651 8580

Historical sites
历史景点

Beamless Hall
无梁殿 Wuliang Dian
地址：紫金山麓
电话：025-8444 6111

Bell Tower
大钟亭 Dazhong Ting
地址：鼓楼区大钟亭 1 号
电话：025-8360 9579

Chaotian Palace
朝天宫 Chaotian Gong
地址：朝天宫 4 号
电话：025-8421 9704

Cock-crow Temple
鸡鸣寺 Jiming Si
地址：鸡鸣寺路 1 号
电话：025-5771 5595

夫子庙 Fuzi Miao
电话：025-8662 8639

Dongling Tomb
东陵墓 Dongling Mu

Drum Tower
鼓楼公园 Gulou Gongyuan
地址：南京鼓楼街
电话：025-8330 1101

First Nanjing Bridge
南京第一长江大桥
Nanjing Diyi ChangJiang Daqiao
地址：宝塔桥东街 7 号
电话：025-8878 2424

Gao Ershi Memorial
高二适纪念馆
Gao Ershi Jinian Guan
地址：浦口区珠江镇
电话：025-5888 2034

Gaochun Old Street
高淳老街 Gaochun Laojie
地址：高淳县淳溪镇高淳老街
电话：025-5733 0559

Imperial Examination Hall
江南贡院 Jiangnan Gongyuan
地址：金陵路 1 号
电话：025-8662 6556

Jinghai Temple
静海寺 Jinghai Si
地址：朝月楼 116 号
电话：025-5880 2973

John Rabe Research and Exchange Center for Peace and Reconciliation
“拉贝故居 / 拉贝与国际安全区纪念馆”和“拉贝和平与冲突化解研究交流中心” Labei Guju
地址：广州路 1 号
电话：025-8359 7227，8368 6306

Li Xiangjun Residence
李香君故居 Lixiangjun Guju
地址: 钞库街 38 号
电话：025-52201692

Lin Sanzhi Memorial
林散之纪念馆 Lin Sanzhi Jinian Guan
地址: 浦口区珠江镇
电话：025-5888 2034

Linggu Pagoda
灵谷塔 Linggu Ta
地址：紫金山麓
电话：025-8444 6111

Liuhe Mosque
六合清真寺 Liuhe Qingzhensi
地址：六合区
电话：025-5775 9741

Nanjing Massacre Memorial Hall
南京大屠杀遇难同胞纪念馆
Nanjing Datusha Yunan Tongbao Jinianguan
地址：水西门外大街 418 号
电话：025-8661 2230

Ming Palace Ruins
明故宫遗址 Ming Gugong Yizhi
地址: 明故宫路
电话：025-8480 3110

Mochou Lake
莫愁湖 Mochou Hu
地址:北门（汉中门大街 35 号）
南门（水西门大街 15 号）
电话：025-8666 1790

Plum Village
梅园新村纪念馆
Meiyuan Xincun Jinian Guan
地址: 汉府街 18-1 号
电话：025-8454 2362

Presidential Palace
总统府 Zhongtongfu
地址:长江路 292 号
电话：025-8457 8788

Qixia Temple
栖霞寺 Qixia Si

地址：栖霞山栖霞街88号
电话：025-8576 1831

Rain Flower Pavilion
雨花台风景区 Yuhuatai FengJingQu
地址: 雨花台215号
电话：025-52411526

Rain Flower Terrace Martyr's Museum
雨花台烈士陵园
Yuhuatai Lieshi Lingyuan
地址: 雨花台215号
电话：025-52411526

River-crossing Victory Memorial
渡江胜利纪念馆
Dujiang Shengli Jinian Guan
地址：中山北路457号挹江门城楼
电话：025-5880 6337

Southern Tang Emperors Tombs
南唐二陵 Nantang Er'Ling
地址：祖堂山西南麓

Stone City
石头城 Shitou Cheng
地址：虎踞路87号
电话：025-8338 3180

Sun Yat-sen Mausoleum
中山陵 Zhongshan Ling
地址：钟山小茅山南麓
电话：025-8443 2799

Tianfei Temple
天妃宫 Tianfei Gong
地址：建宁路284号
电话：025-5859 1740

Tiansheng Natural Bridge
天生桥 Tianshen Qiao
地址：溧水县城西部
电话：025- 5722 5656

Wang-Xie Residence
王谢故居 WangXie GuJu
地址:乌衣巷9号
电话：025-5223 1693

Gan Xi Residence Museum
甘熙故居 GanXi GuJu
地址：中山南路南捕厅15号
电话：025-5221 7104, 5225 6297

Xiaoling Tomb Complex
孝陵墓 XiaoLing Mu
地址:紫金山麓
电话：025-8444 6111

Xiao Xian Memorial
萧娴纪念馆 Xiao xian JiNianGuan
地址: 浦口区珠江镇
电话：025-5888 2034

Xuanwu Lake
玄武湖 XuanWu Hu
地址：玄武巷1号
电话：025-83347373

Yangshan Stele
阳山碑材 Yangshan BeiCai
地址: 江宁区汤山镇古泉村宁杭公路旁
电话：025-8411 0582

Zheng He Tomb
郑和纪念墓 Zhenghe Jinian Mu
地址：牛首山南麓
电话：025-8613 8528

Zheng He Treasure-Ship Shipyard
郑和宝船遗址 Zhenghe Baochuan Yizhi
地址：滨江路 57 号
电话：025-8622 7011

Zhonghua Gate
中华门 Zhonghua Men
地址：中华门
电话：025-8662 5752

Museums 博物馆

City Museum of Nanjing (Chaotian Palace)
南京市朝天宫博物馆
Nanjing Chaotiangong Bowuguan
地址：朝天宫 4 号
电话：025-8421 9709

Folk-custom Museum (Jiangxin Island)
南京民俗博物馆
Nanjing Minsu Bowuguan
地址：中山南路南捕厅 19 号
电话：025-5221 7104

Gaochun Ancient Brick-carving Museum
高淳砖雕博物馆
Gaochun Zhuandiao Bowuguan
地址：高淳县淳溪镇高淳老街
电话：025-5733 0559

Gaochun Folk Customs Exhibition Hall
高淳民俗博物馆
Gaochun Minsu Bowuguan
地址：高淳县淳溪镇高淳老街
电话：025-5733 0559

Heavenly Kingdom History Museum
太平天国历史博物馆
Taiping Tianguo Lishi Bowuguan
地址：瞻园路 128 号
电话：025-5220 1849

Jiangsu Provincial Museum (Nanjing Museum)
江苏省博物馆（南京博物院）
Jiangsu Sheng Bowuguan (Nanjing Bowuyuan)
地址：中山东路 321 号
电话：025-8480 2119

Ming City Wall History Museum
南京明城垣历史博物馆
Nanjing MingchengYuan
Lishi Bowuguan
地址：解放门8号
电话：025-8360 8359, 8361 6305

Nanjing History Museum
南京历史博物馆
Nanjing Lishi Bowuguan
地址：中山东路321号
电话：025-8480 2119

Nanjing Treaty History Museum
(Jinghai Temple)
《南京条约》史料陈列馆
《Nanjing Tiaoyue》 Shiliao Chenlie Guan
地址：朝月楼116号
电话：025-5880 2973

Paleontology Museum
南京古生物博物馆
Nanjing Gushengwu Bowuguan
地址：北京东路39号
电话：025-8328 2253,8328 2254

Rain Flower Pebble Museum
雨花石博物馆
Yuahua Shi Bowuguan
地址：雨花台215号
电话：025-5241 1526

Yuejiang Tower
阅江楼 Yuejiang Lou
地址：建宁路202号
电话：025-5881 5369

Parks, Gardens and Other Green Spaces 公园

Bailu Zhou Park
白鹭洲公园 Bailuzhou Gongyuan
地址：秦淮区白鹭村1号
电话：025-8370 4919

Fujiabian Hacienda
傅家边庄园 Fujiabian ZhuangYuan
地址：溧水县洪蓝镇
电话：025-5743 0340

Golden Ox Lake
金牛湖 Jinniu Hu
地址：六合区八百桥镇金牛村
电话：025-5756 6878

Hongshan Zoological Park
红山森林动物园
Hongshan SengLin Dongwu Yuan
地址：小红山
电话：025-8562 0178

Jiuhua Hill
九华山 Jiuhua Shan
地址：北京东路九华山庄
电话：025-8321 3373

Pearl Spring (Zhenzhu) Park
珍珠泉公园 ZhenzhuQuan Gongyuan
地址：浦口区珍珠街
电话：025-5860 1545

Purple Clouds Lake
紫霞湖 Zixia Hu
地址：明孝陵旁

Qingliang Hill
清凉山 Qingliang Shan
地址：清凉山 83 号
电话：025-8372 8012

Stone Pillar Forest
石柱林 Shizhu Lin
地址：六合区桂子山东北处

Swallow Rock
燕子矶 Yanzi Ji
地址：栖霞山燕子矶临江街 3 号
电话：025-8531 1337

Tangshan Hot Spring
汤山温泉 Tangshan Wenquan
地址：江宁区汤山镇
电话：025-8410 3031

White Horse Park
白马公园 Baima Gongyuan
地址：玄武区白马山庄 1 号
电话：025-8540 8062

Wuchaomen Park
午朝门公园 Wuchaomen Gongyuan
电话：025-8461 1262

Wulong Pond Garden
乌龙潭公园 Wulongtan Gongyuan
地址：广州路 217 号
电话：025-8370 4910

Xiuqiu Park
绣球公园 Xiuqiu Gongyuan
地址：中山北路 406 号
电话：025-5875 5365

Xuanwu Lake
玄武湖 Xuanwu Hu
地址：玄武巷 1 号
电话：025-8337 4373

Xuyuan Garden
煦园（即总统府西花园）
地址：长江路 292 号
电话：025-8664 1131

Yaodang Ecological Tourist Village
瑶宕村旅游农业观光中心
Yaodangcun Nongye Guanguang Zhongxin
地址：瑶宕村

Yinghu Peach Garden Tourist and Vacation Area
迎湖桃园 Yinghu Taoyuan
地址：高淳县阳江镇
电话：025-5780 8717

Youzi Mountain
游子山庄 Youzi Shanzhuang
地址：高淳县东坝镇游子山庄
电话：025-5785 1427

Zheng He Park
郑和公园 Zhenghe Gongyuan
地址：太平巷35号
电话：025-8451 2884

Zhan Garden
瞻园 Zhanyuan
地址：瞻园路128号
电话：025-822 01849

Shopping 购物

Chaotian Palace Market
朝天宫古玩市场
ChaoTianGong Guwan ShiChang
地址：朝天宫4号
电话：025-8420 0177，8446 6460

Nanjing Handcraft Center
南京工艺美术中心
Nanjing Gongyi Meishu Zhongxin
地址：北京东路31号
电话：025-8771 1574

Jinying International Shopping Center
金鹰国际购物中心
JinYing Guoji Gouwu Zhongxin
地址：汉中路89号
电话：025-8470 8899

Jiangsu Relics Store
江苏文物商店
Jiangsu Wenwu Shangdian
地址：中山东路321号
电话：025-8480 0701

Nanjing Store
南京商厦 Nanjing Shangsha
地址：龙蟠路2号
电话：025-8550 5637

Taiping Store
太平商场 Taiping Shangchang
地址：太平南路279号
电话：025-8440 2050

Bibliography

（参考文献）

Bird, Isabella. *The Yangtze Valley and Beyond*. London: Virago Press, 1985.

Brodsky, Joseph. *On Grief and Reason*. New York: Farrar, Straus and Giroux, 1997.

Brook, Timothy, ed. *Documents on the Rape of Nanjing*. Ann Arbor: University of Michigan Press, 1999.

Buck, Pearl. *The Good Earth*. New York: Grosset & Dunlap, 1933.

Cody, Jeffrey. *Building in China: Henry K. Murphy's "Adaptive Architecture", 1914-1935.* Hong Kong: Chinese University Press, 2001.

Chang, Iris. *The Rape of Nanking*. New York: Penguin USA, 1998.

Cheng, J.C. *Chinese Sources for the Taiping Rebellion, 1850-1864*. Hong Kong: Hong Kong University Press, 1963.

"Dawn of the Chinese Civilization: Jades of the Liangzhu Culture." Art Museum. The Chinese University of Hong Kong, 1999.

Fogel, Joshua, ed. *The Nanjing Massacre in History and Historiography*. Berkeley: University of California Press, 2000.

Hessler, Peter. *Oracle Bones*. New York: HarperCollins, 2006.

Knapp, Ronald G. *China's Walled Cities*. Hong Kong: Oxford University Press, 2000.

Kong Shangren. *The Peach Blossom Fan*. Adapted by Chen Meilin. Kuang Peihua, Ren Lingjuan and He Fei, trans. Beijing: New World Press, 2001.

Kristof, Nicholas D. "1492: The Prequel." *The New York Times*, June 6, 1999.

Levathes, Louise. *When China Ruled the Seas*. New York: Oxford University Press, 1994.

Li Po. *Selected Poems of Li Po*. David Hinton, trans. New York: New Directions, 1998.

Lu Yanzhi. "Memorials to Dr. Sun Yat-sen in Nanking and Canton." *Far Eastern Review*, Issue 25, 1929.

Maisels, Charles. *Early Civilizations of the Old World*. New York: Routeledge, 1999.

Menzies, Gavin. *1421: The Year China Discovered the World*. London: Bantam Books, 2002.

Mote, Frederick W. "The Transformation of Nanking, 1350-1400." In *The City in Late Imperial China*, ed. G. William Skinner. Stanford: Stanford University Press, 1977.

The New Directions Anthology of Classical Chinese Poetry. New York: New Directions, 2003. Translation of Li Bai's "Ch'ang-kan Village Song" by David Hinton.

Paludan, Ann. *Chronicle of the Chinese Emperors*. London: Thames and Hudson, 1998.

Peck, Graham. *Two Kinds of Time*. Boston: Houghton Mifflin Company, 1967.

Phillips, Kerk. "A Concise History of the City of Nanjing: How it Relates to the City You See Today." Working paper.

The Poems of Li Bai. http://chinese-poems.com/lbe.html. Translation of "Changgan Memories" by Mark Alexander.

Pomfret, John. *Chinese Lessons*. New York: Henry Holt and Co., 2006.

Rabe, John. *The Good Man of Nanking*. John E. Woods, translator. New York: Random House, 1998.

Spence, Jonathan D. *The Gate of Heavenly Peace: The Chinese and Their Revolution, 1895-1980*. New York: Viking Penguin, 1981.

Spence, Jonathan D. *God's Chinese Son: The Taiping Heavenly Kingdom of Hong Xiuquan*. New York & London: W. W. Norton & Co., 1996.

Spence, Jonathan D. *The Search for Modern China*. New York: W.W. Norton and Co., 1991.

Su Tong. *My Life as Emperor*. Howard Goldblatt, translator. London: Faber and Faber, 1992.

Su Tong. *Raise the Red Lantern*. Michael S. Duke, translator. London: Simon and Schuster, 2000.

Theroux, Paul. *Sailing Through China*. Boston: Houghton Mifflin, 1984.

Till, Barry with Paula Swart. *In Search of Old Nanking*. Hong Kong: Joint Publishing Co., 1982.

Twitchett, Denis & Frederick W. Mote, eds. Vol. 8 of *The Cambridge History of China*. Cambridge: Cambridge University Press, 1998.

Wagner, Rudolf G. *Reenacting the Heavenly Vision*. Berkeley: University of California Institute of East Asian Studies, 1984.

Wang Qianhua, ed. *Xiaoling Tomb of the Ming Dynasty*. Nanjing: Nanjing Press, 2004.

Winchester, Simon. *The River at the Center of the World: A Journey up the Yangtze, and Back in Chinese Time*. New York: Henry Holt and Co., 2004.

Xu Huping. *The Treasures of the Nanjing Museum*. Hong Kong: London Editions, 2001.

Xu Huping, ed. *Gems of Collections in the Nanjing Museum*, Vols 1-10. Shanghai: Chinese Classics Publishing House, 1997.

Ye Zhaoyan. *Old Nanjing: Reflections of Scenes on the Qinhuai River.* Beijing: Foreign Languages Press, 2003.

Zhang Lijia & Calum MacLeod. *China Remembers*. Hong Kong: Oxford University Press, 1999.

Zhu Chenshan, Ed. *The Picture Collection of Nanjing Massacre and International Rescue*. Nanjing: Jiangsu Ancient Book Publishing House, 2002.

Index

(索引)

T

V

W

X

Y

Z

编委会名单

Advance Praise for *China Through the Looking Glass, Nanjing*
国际名人谈《深度看中国·南京》

"For any traveler, student, teacher, or resident in Nanjing, Roy Kesey's book is an invaluable guide to what could otherwise be an overwhelming amount of sites to see.He gives unbiased information, logically presented in a compact and readable format, allowing readers to gain a firm grasp on the history and culture of one of the world's great historic capitals without being bombarded by facts. Recommended as required reading for before, during, and after a visit to any of Nanjing's sites."
相对于南京丰富的旅游看点，Roy Kesey 的这本书对任何人而言都是一本非常有价值的指南书，不论游客、学生、老师，还是南京人。他的文风简洁而饶有趣味。通过对史实公正而理性的展示，让读者勿需恶补相关知识很容易就抓住并了解了古都南京深厚的历史和文化，而这座城市曾经是世界上最伟大的首都！
强烈推荐本书为南京的旅游必读书，不管是在去之前，在旅途中或是旅游之后。
Julie Sisk, editor, *MAP Magazine*

"In this well-informed and beautifully observed book, Nanjing at last has a guide worthy of its rich history and contemporary vibrancy. An elegant, engaging writer, Roy Kesey is the ideal guide to the mighty city on the Yangtze. His book avoids potted recitation of facts in favor of compelling historical anecdotes, scholarly quotes, and profiles of historical figures that breathe life into Nanjing's many tourist sites and inform its unique modern character. Leavened with humor and telling details, this book should inspire many visits to Nanjing."
南京终于有了一本与她丰富历史和现代活力相匹配、融信息俱全和文笔优美为一体的指南书。一位年轻有为，极富魅力的作家，Roy Kesey 是这座长江边上的城市最好的向导。他的书避开了对现实单调的复述，而是热衷于历史轶事、文人学术、历史人物传记，并给南京的众多旅游景点注入生命，从而形成独特的现代风格。这本（兼）带幽默风格和详细资讯的书，会鼓励更多游客来南京旅游。
- Adam Pillsbury, Editor of *The Insider's Guide to Beijing* and *Beijing Excursion Guide*

"I can't imagine anyone better suited than Roy Kesey to present Nanjing to the world. Focusing on the city's long history and vibrant cultural scene, and possessed of the 'magic talent of releasing flowers from his pen,' Kesey portrays the city vividly. As he notes, the mythological animal known as the bixie, with its head raised proudly to heaven, is the key to understanding the past and present of Nanjing. Both visitors and armchair travelers will find this book a joy to read."
我不能想象还有哪位作家比Roy Kesey更合适把南京介绍给世界了。立足于这座城市的悠久历史和令人震撼的文化，作家Kesey妙笔生花，给我们描绘了一幅生动的城市画面。也正如他所说，那个傲然昂头向苍穹的神兽蜒避邪，是一把了解南京过去和现在最好的钥匙。不管是旅行家还是喜欢通过看书来获得旅行感受的读者来说，都会在这本书里发现乐趣。
- Zhang Lijia, Author of *Frog in a Well* and co-author of *China Remembers*

"Nanjing was the first city in China that I ever visited and it left a deep impression on me. This book captures many of the first and subsequent impressions that I gained of this great city of Nanjing, the Southern Capital of China on the mighty Yangtze River. It is great to see the *City of Universal Love* or *Bo Ai* from a Westerner's viewpoint. The author has done a fabulous job of researching the city's history, culture and attractions. It's a feast of information on one of China's greatest tourist cities."
"南京是我所到的第一个中国城市，她给我留下了深刻的印象。这本书包含了很多我对于南京这座位于雄伟的长江边上的中国南方的伟大城市的最初以及后来的印象。从一个西方人的视角来看这座博爱之都是一件很了不起的事情。作者对南京的历史、文化和风景名胜进行了深入细致的研究。这本书是关于中国最伟大的旅游城市之一的信息盛宴。"

阿拉斯泰尔.莫里森教授，美国印第安那州西拉法叶是普渡大学旅游管理特级教授，著有《旅游与旅游营销》、《旅游体系》和《旅游：世界的桥梁》

Professor Alastair Morrison, Distinguished Professor of Hospitality and Tourism Management, Purdue University, West Lafayette, Indiana, USA and author of *Hospitality and Travel Marketing*, *The Tourism System*, and *Tourism: Bridges across Continents.*

图书在版编目(CIP)数据

南京 = Nanjing:英文 / 骆一康著.—北京：原子能出版社，2007.4
ISBN 978-7-5022-3876-6

Ⅰ.南… Ⅱ.骆… Ⅲ.南京市—概况—英文 Ⅳ.K925.31

中国版本图书馆 CIP 数据核字(2007)第 024211 号

主办：南京市旅游局
承办：国际作家俱乐部(The International Writers Club)
　　　《深度看中国》系列书编委会
　　　北京迈萃文化传播有限公司
总　策　划：陈　刚
编委会主任：许　宏
执行总策划：权新颖
地址：北京市朝阳区建国路壹线国际 C2-703
电话：1371 8809 877　010-596709441　010-596709442
邮箱：bjmatric@163.com
南京旅游咨询热线：025-5226 9008
网址：Http://www.nju.gov.cn

NANJING

出版发行：原子能出版社（北京市海滨区阜成路 43 号 邮编：100037）
责任编辑：谭　俊
印　　刷：北京雅彩印刷有限责任公司
经　　销：全国新华书店
开　　本：787mm × 1092mm　1/32
印　　张：12
字　　数：350 千字
版　　次：2007 年 4 月北京第 1 版　2007 年 4 月北京第 1 次印刷
书　　号：ISBN 978-7-5022-3876-6
印　　数：1—5000
定　　价：RMB: 100.00　USD: 19.80
